Club Pro Guy's Other Black Book

WISDOM FROM A LIFETIME
OF PUNCHING OUT SIDEWAYS

Club Pro Guy
with Paul Koehorst

Foreword by Scott McCarron

Club Pro Guy Books
Kansas City, Missouri

Club Pro Guy's Other Black Book
by Club Pro Guy with Paul Koehorst

Copyright © 2021 by Club Pro Guy LLC
All rights reserved. No part of this book may be reproduced or transmitted in any form by any means, electronic, mechanical, photocopying, recording or otherwise, without written permission of the author.

Cover design and book design by Northern Pine Design.
Library of Congress Control Number: 2021917506

International Standard Book Number: 978-1-7376697-0-8
Printed in the United States of America.

"This book was written to help golfers of all skill levels improve their game. If it doesn't make you a better golfer, that's 100% on you."

—Club Pro Guy
Kansas City, Missouri
2021

Contents

Foreword by Scott McCarron	ix
Introduction	1
The Big Choice	11
Knowing Your Role on a Buddies Trip	12
Lesson Packages	16
What Are You Hitting?	16
My Favorite Things	17
Work Harder, or Don't	19
Putt Better Fast!	19
Charity Scrambles	20
The Small Pocket	23
How to Practice	23
Playing under the Influence	26
Strategy	30
Thanks, but No Thanks	30
My Ten Bucket-List Courses	31
Using Analytics to Improve Your Putting	34
Better Short Than Weak	35
Which Tee Box Is Right for You?	35
Gripping the Club	38
The Secret of the Golf Swing—I've Figured It Out!!!	39
The Pre-Shot Routine	39
Save It for When It Counts	42

Travel on Tour	43
Red Light and Green Light Pins	43
Always Snip the Red Wire	46
Club Romance	47
My 10 Rules for Punching Out Sideways	48
Advice I Hope You Never Have to Use	55
Being a Teacher	55
The Dewsweepers	58
So True	59
On-Course Bathroom Strategy	60
Odd Jobs	62
The Business of Golf	63
Leave the Dockers at Home	65
Five Things Parents of Young Golfers Should Know	66
(Miss It, Miss It, Miss It)	68
Augusta National and the Masters	68
The 747 Swing Thought System®	77
Glory Days	80
Listening to Your Body	80
"What'd Ya Shoot?"	81
Real Money Players	83
Course Marshals	83
Golf's Toughest Shot	86
Dating Strippers	87
How to Win Every Rules Dispute	88
The Key to Alignment	89
Pre-Round Preparation	89

The Most Overrated Accomplishment in Golf	92
My Faith	93
Elevating Your Game Is Overrated	94
Always Go for It	95
Playing with Women	96
Caddie Breakups	101
The Evolution of the Golf Swing	101
The Rule That's Killing Golf (and Why You Should Break It)	102
A Keen Eye for (Lack-of) Talent	104
Assigning Proper Blame	105
Trying to "Make It"	107
Are You Good Enough to Get Angry?	108
My Lesson with El Chapo	110
Merchandising	111
The Dreaded Fried Egg - Time to Cook Up an Excuse	112
A Lesson in Lessons	114
How I Make Money	115
The Dreaded Slice	117
Provisionals	118
Music on the Course	119
My Private Cache of Swing Thoughts	120
The Retired Member Guy	123
Taking an Inventory of Your Game	125
Growing the Game	125
The Right Shaft May Be the Wrong Shaft	127
Management 101	127

Pick It Up or Putt It?	128
Private Country Club Etiquette	128
Endorsements	131
Is Custom Fitting Right for You?	133
Money Talks	133
A Game of Honor	134
My Eight-Hole Par Streak	135
Lesson Terminology	135
Getting "Comfortable" with Training Aids	137
A Day in the Life	139
Match Play Mindset	140
Getting the Most out of Playing by Yourself	140
Staying Cool When Going Low	142
How to Carry Yourself on the Golf Course	143
The Power of Language in Match Play	145
Developing a Go-To Shot	147
Playing in the Zone	147
Fighting the First-Tee Jitters	148
The Camera Doesn't Lie	150
Picking the Right Putter	150
The Difference between Tour Pros and Club Pros	152
What to Expect for Your Golfing Dollar	154
Calculating Your True Score®	157
Fueling Your Body	159
Avoiding Blow-Up Holes	161
The Most Valuable Chapter in This Book	163
Where I Go from Here	165
Photos	168

Foreword
By Scott McCarron

My journey to the big show was not unique. Like Club Pro Guy, I too played some of the top minitours, such as the California Tour, the Golden State Tour, the Canadian Tour, and my favorite—the Hooters Tour. CPG would have been perfect for that tour! I learned so much back then, like: don't rent a compact car for $33 bucks a day when you can rent a U-HAUL for $19.95; if you carry a big dead spider around, you can get a discount off your room when you show it to the hotel's general manager; and if you take your courtesy car to the strip club, always park in the back so the tournament sponsors don't see it. Little things like that can make you or break you when chasing your dream to make it on the PGA Tour.

There's a razor-thin margin between a life of private jets and paid appearances or folding shirts and teaching golf camps to 50 kids who hate your guts.

Although I'm grateful that I'm one of the lucky few who made it to the big time, I'm also forever bonded with the guys like CPG who came up just short.

When I finally became an established player on the PGA Tour, I often heard rumors about a guy that was just killing it on the Mexican Mini-Tour. It wasn't that he was winning everything, because he clearly wasn't. It was the stories of his swashbuckling punch-out game, his dogged determination to play U.S. Kids equipment due to the small print in his endorsement contract, and especially his eight-hole par streak, which became the stuff of legend. To this day, it's difficult for anyone in the world of golf to talk about El Chapo's Taint without mentioning how his streak came to an end there.

I finally got to meet CPG a few years ago in Florida at the Players Championship. It was that chance encounter that changed my game forever. I was a competitor in the field and he was in town accompanying his then girlfriend, Tawny Ray, as she worked a three-day stint at Pinky's Gentleman's Club in nearby Jacksonville. At that particular time, I was looking to revamp my swing in preparation for the PGA Champions Tour and was intrigued with what I had read about CPG's proprietary 747 Swing Thought System.®

We met at a Chili's near the Stadium Course where he spent the first 90 minutes of the conversation trying to dump his Branson timeshare on me. However, midway through his eighth Zima, he began to hand me the keys to the kingdom. His actual explanation of the 747 Swing Thought System made my head spin, but it got me thinking. If I can just fill my head with a countless barrage of swing thoughts at once, it would overload my brain and it would just be quiet.

Three short years later, I won the Charles Schwab Cup and the rest is history! It's all still a work in progress, and I'm constantly having to add in new swing thoughts or subtract swing thoughts based on the tournament, the day or the swing. But when I'm under the gun, I stick to the key principle, which is to aim way right and double-cross it. As long as I flip it at the bottom, it's going to go where I'm not looking.

Think of this book as your own little one-on-one with CPG, without the coffee breath and the nonstop requests to borrow money. These teachings come around only once in a lifetime, and I not only believe you will enjoy reading this book but I also think it will become a reference manual for golfers of all ages and abilities for generations to come. CPG will teach you about alignment (which means nothing), how to win at all costs, using provisional balls to your advantage, how to always prepare for the worst, and much more!

I would not be where I am today without many of these wise teachings. I'm just grateful that CPG didn't make it on tour so he could share his knowledge with the world instead of using it to kick my ass. Take my word for it, after reading this book, you'll use your old instructional books to line the cat litter box. Long live Club Pro Guy.

Introduction

SEVERAL YEARS AGO I was giving a playing lesson to a young junior student here at the Club. We'll call him "Billy" for the purpose of protecting his anonymity, but his real name is Griffin Brownfield, and he was a total pain in the ass. Like most junior players who experience a small amount of success at a young age, Billy had delusions of grandeur when it came to his golf career. Despite being in elementary school, he honestly thought he was destined to play on the PGA Tour and would not shut up about it.

As an elite club professional who spent years on tour, I did not share Billy's optimism, and felt I had a responsibility to temper his expectations. I would often remind him that he had better odds of winning *American Idol* or having a threesome with a pair of supermodels than he did of walking the fairways of the PGA Tour. He wouldn't listen. Billy was naive, stubborn and full of himself, even for a fifth grader.

Like most playing lessons I conduct with junior students, I needed a little "juice" to make it worth my time. Billy and I were playing a standard $20 Nassau with one-down automatic presses. On this particular day, Billy was hanging tight with me. I won the first hole when I picked up a six-footer that I "mistakenly" thought Billy said was "good," as well as the second hole when I called a penalty on Billy for having the "slope" feature activated on his range finder. After halving holes three thru six with bogeys, Billy won holes seven and eight with gritty pars, setting up the par-4 ninth as the hole where everything would be decided.

Billy teed off first and ripped one down the right side and found the long rough near the hazard. Sensing an opening, I reached back for a little extra, but ended up hitting a little heely-cut down the center of the fairway roughly 20 yards behind Billy. After a forgettable approach shot short and left of the green, I rushed over to help Billy in his ball search, due to the fact that I did not fully trust him.

I initiated my standard routine of good-sportsmanship-theater by looking for my opponent's ball in an area where I was certain not to find it and making overt statements like, "who's got a stopwatch?" After feeling like I had sufficiently gone through the motions, I decided I had done enough and walked back to my cart. As I was about to exit the rough, to my great surprise, I noticed a Titleist Pro V1x with Billy's distinctive smiley face markings right below me.

I reflexively shouted, "found one," which looking back was probably a mistake. Had I been thinking clearly, I would have simply stepped on the ball and finished running out the clock until Billy declared the ball lost and went back to the tee to re-hit. That would have meant almost certain victory on the hole as well as a tidy profit on the day's action. Instead, Billy perked up and began to walk toward me. Panicked, but trying not to show it, I calmly asked Billy what ball he was playing and he responded by saying it was a Titleist 3 Pro V1x with smiley face markings. In a move that would be worthy of an Academy Award nomination, I replied by calmly saying, "Oh sorry, this is a Lady Noodle with a big mower gash in it," as I threw the ball deep into the hazard.

What I thought was the end of the story certainly was not as the ball hit a small, yet sturdy branch on a tree across the creek and miraculously ricocheted back toward us before coming to rest at Billy's feet. As Billy picked up the ball, I could see the look of confusion and astonishment on his face as he began to put together the pieces of what was happening. When it fully hit him, his disappointment was impossible to hide and he broke down in tears.

When the round was over we sat down in the clubhouse to talk about what he had just learned. I ordered Billy a lemonade and got myself three beers, four hotdogs and a pretzel and charged it all to his dad's account. After collecting my winnings, I explained to Billy how he had just learned the hard way the consequences of picking up a ball to identify it before calling over a rules official. I reminded him how it only cost him $60 today, but on the PGA Tour, a mistake like that could be worth hundreds of thousands of dollars.

As Billy sat in silence and slowly nursed his lemonade, I wasn't sure if he was more upset about his obvious rules infraction or the fact that he had just lost a month's allowance. With the buzz from my third beer starting to hit me, I found myself looking deep into his watery eyes, where my mind began to wander, and I began to think back to when I was Billy's age.

I was born in Kansas City, Missouri, in the mid-70s when professional golf was at its absolute pinnacle. My mom, Debbie, was a professional golf "groupie" and would travel from tour stop to tour stop with her friend Cheyenne in the hopes of getting their claws into the next Hubert Green or Bob Murphy.

In August of 1973, somewhere between the Greater Hartford Open and the Westchester Classic, my mom decided to swing by a mini-tour event to scout some future stars. That's where she met my father, Dale Guy. At that time, Dale had conditional status on the 3-Mile Island Tour in Pennsylvania thanks to his breakout season on the Aleutian Islands Tour in Alaska the season before. One glance was all it took. I was conceived 45-minutes later in the restroom of a Harrisburg Amoco Station.

I love my mom, but it's no surprise Dale began to play poorly after knocking her up. The responsibility of a new child, coupled with her constant nagging, was not a great recipe for success. She used to say things to him like "why can't you putt like Jim Colbert?" or "I heard Tom Watson bought his wife Linda a Trans-Am."

The pressure was too much. Dale went on to lose his status, virtually ending his dreams of making it to the show. In the years that followed he bounced around from tour to tour desperately searching for his big break. Tragically, he died two years later when he succumbed to hypothermia during a Monday qualifier at the Yukon Tour's season opening "Ice Breaker Four-Ball" in extreme Northern Canada.

Although I have no memory of him, I always felt Dale's presence as my mom and I continued to travel the country digging for PGA Tour gold. As a starry-eyed kid who was just starting to pick up the game, I wouldn't trade those days for anything. That life exposed me to a "who's who" of legendary players as they stopped by for 30 or even 60 minutes to "hang out" in the back of the RV with my mom and/or Cheyenne. I can't name names but more than half the members of the PGA Tour Hall of Fame must have paid a visit to what became known as "The Other Tour Truck." I think it was a lot like what Ken Griffey Jr. must have felt like spending time in a major league clubhouse as a kid with his dad, except for the fact that his dad didn't have to have sex with anyone.

As for my mom, she retired as a groupie in 1987, after accomplishing her lifelong goal of spending a night with Fuzzy Zoeller. There's a certain amount of satisfaction that comes along with going out on top and mom achieved that. Both figuratively and literally.

As for golf, I was a bit of a late bloomer. After a second team all-conference campaign my junior year at Hickman Mills High School in Kansas City, my senior year was cut short by injuries and suspensions. A bout with undiagnosed ADHD, coupled with a string of alleged on-course cheating issues, scared off several potential college coaches. Looking back, it was probably for the best. I innately knew I was ready to turn pro. After a disappointing 96-90-WD in First Stage of PGA Tour Q-School, I decided to take my talents south of the border and ply my trade on the Mexican Mini-Tour.

I could probably write an entire book, or maybe even a volume of books, on my time in Mexico, but I'll just take a moment to hit the high points. It's a career that spanned 14 years and produced 18 made cuts, three wives, six DUIs and an eight-hole par streak that essentially defined a generation of golfers south of the border. I cashed three-figure checks at prestigious events like the Yucatan Masters, the Matamoros Four-Ball and the Coacalco de Barriozabal Modified Stableford. I battled El Chapo's Taint, beat a paternity suit from a Cabo San Lucas motel maid, and put 560,000 miles on a 1990 Mazda Miata that I'm still making payments on to this day.

Like all great runs, there comes that moment when you realize it's over. For me, it was at the 2002 season ending Mezcal Shootout, where I shot 94-102 to miss the cut by 56. That event was also marred by a physical altercation I had with a young boy who was in attendance representing Mexico's version of The First Tee Foundation. It was then that I finally realized I was no longer able to maintain the elite-level of excellence that I had become accustomed to. Not only was my body starting to break down, but I was beginning to notice players half my age burst onto the scene with the ability to break 80 almost at will. It was time to step aside.

Like so many athletes who are suddenly forced to leave the white-hot spotlight of professional sports, retirement was difficult for me. I naively thought the transition from the golf course to the boardroom would be a seamless one. It wasn't. After getting turned down for several C-Suite level positions on Wall Street, I took a sales position at the Nevada Bob's in Lubbock, Texas, and began to realize that golf was in my blood. I needed to get back in the game.

After splashing my resume out to several semi-private clubs and upper-end driving ranges throughout the Midwest seeking a head professional position, I received multiple (two) offers. In an effort to be closer to my mom, I turned down a more lucrative opportunity in Sioux City, Iowa, and settled on the club I am at now in Kansas City, Missouri.

In the nearly two decades since, I have established myself as one of the most influential club pros in the nation. My instructional resume includes the development of the 747 Swing Thought System®, the Stack & Jilt Short Game Method, and various handicap manipulation techniques. My students have captured nine (net) club championships and I produced a VHS instructional series on "The Secret" to punching out sideways that was widely distributed in Central America, but never quite got off the ground here in the States. However, I'm probably most proud of the work I've done with single and divorced moms. Some teachers focus on beginners, or juniors, or even tour players. My sweet spot is with MILFs and I wouldn't trade my time with these women for the world because it's an area where I'm able to make a real impact.

As I look back on the day Billy slid that $60 across the table to pay me for the bet he lost during our playing lesson, I'm reminded how blessed I've been since my playing career ended. Sure, there were a few rough patches along the way, but look at me now. Not only do I still play to a high, single-digit index, but I also make $42,000 a year, drive a 1990 Mazda Miata, own a timeshare in Branson, and enjoy a very loose reciprocal agreement with the owner of a nearby strip club, Bottoms Up.

Now is not the time to get comfortable. I'm often reminded of what my longtime idol and Tour legend Jay Don Blake once said, "With great success comes great responsibility." That's a mantra I live by, and it's the inspiration and driving force behind this book.

I have learned and experienced so much over the last four decades that it would not be fair to those who came before me or those just now discovering the game if I didn't document that information for the world to see. That's what this "other" Black Book is all about. Giving back. I hope you allow the treasures written within these pages to not only help you become a better golfer, but a better human being.

All My Best!
Club Pro Guy

The Big Choice

ANYONE WHO WANTS to shoot in the 70s consistently, has to make what I call, "The Big Choice." Do you want to be married or do you want to play good golf? You can't do both. To be a player who consistently shoots in the 70s takes tons of practice, playing multiple times a week and investing major dough on clubs, lessons and green fees. All of those activities are the complete opposite of what it takes to be a good husband.

I've been in three marriages and the formula was always the same. When my game was working my marriage suffered, and when my game was suffering my marriage still suffered, because I had a crippling addiction to hookers.

The point is, if you want to be an elite player, either never get married or go ahead and get divorced.

Knowing Your Role on a Buddies Trip

THERE'S NOTHING quite like a buddies golf trip.

Who doesn't love the thought of three days away from the monotony of work, kids, and your mildly overweight wife to go to a golf destination that is typically much better than the muni you play on back home? While I haven't organized a buddies trip since 2007 (when the Mazatlan Madness event I planned was cancelled due to Tropical Storm Humberto and I pocketed everyone's $500 deposit), I'm a veteran of many a boys golf trip and know what it takes for it to go off without a hitch. A big part of that is who you invite and each and every one of those guys doing their part to make it successful. You and your buddies may already be unknowingly playing these roles, but if you're thinking of getting a new crew together for a weekend of golf and shenanigans you need to put the right team together like it's *Oceans 11*.

The Organizer - Deals with all the bullshit including tee times, hotel reservations, van rental and last-minute cancellations because one guy didn't tell his wife he was leaving town until the day before the event. You don't get a single "thank you" for this role, and all the guys who didn't lift a finger are telling you how it could or should have been done better. This job takes strong organizational skills and is generally best suited for accountants, attorneys or stay-at-home dads.

The Straight Arrow - He's the only guy in the group that reads the organizer's emails, knows the scoring format, where you're meeting for dinner, has the keys to the rental van, etc. Call him if you need a ride to the emergency room or if you ate too many edibles and are freaking the fuck out. This is also the only guy who FaceTimes his wife every night and always annoyingly plays "Devil's Advocate" when someone comes up with a plan to invite eight prostitutes to the rental house.

The Accountant - He's got to chase down scorecards, pay out the skins, make sure everyone pays for dinner, etc. Another thankless job that's done only because he doesn't want to get screwed himself. If there are enough side games going on, a good accountant can typically skim enough off the top to get his trip paid for.

Drug Mule - Pretty self-explanatory. Most of you have kids and jobs and can't exactly risk getting caught with an eight-ball in your dopp kit at Chicago O'Hare. This job is usually taken by the young, single guy in the group who typically doesn't have a lot to lose. Your mule probably has a couple of misdemeanors already and transporting some contraband over state lines won't phase him. Want a gummy for around the fire pit? He's got it. Need an Ambien to get to sleep? He's got it. Want to do a couple rails off a stripper's ass? He's got it!

Energy Guy - He boozes, eats, smokes, and parties like his life depends on it. This is the guy who, despite a 7 a.m. tee time, wants to drive 150 miles on a two-lane road to the Canadian border at midnight, because he heard there's a titty bar that allows you to bust a nut. This guy is the heartbeat of the crew. Every trip needs the energy guy to drag the whole group across the finish line.

Guy Who Keeps His Eye on the Energy Guy - The energy guy can scuttle the entire trip if he's not reigned in. If left unattended he can start a brawl, get arrested, or wind up setting a fire in the lobby of your Hampton Inn. "Guy who keeps his eye on the energy guy" is a critical role if your group has any chance of making it to the tee for the Saturday morning alternate shot format.

Single Guy - He owes it to the married guys to share his collection of nudes, show off his Tinder matches and aggressively hit on any women who enter your airspace for the entirety of the weekend.

He's the one who actually has sex with women on the trip while everyone else in the group is talking about having sex with women on the trip. This is the guy everyone in the group envies.

Supply Man - We rely on the supply man to be stocked up on Advil, Tiger Balm, koozies, chewing tobacco, lighters, all that shit, because God knows most of the crew will roll into town totally unprepared. Hopefully he has some sunscreen too.

Boring, Married Golf Guys - You need a few of these. They pay on time. They show up on time. They're there to play golf. They're the connective tissue that keeps the whole thing from falling apart.

If you don't see your role here, you better be buying beers for everyone else every chance you get or entertain the rest of us by eating a whole gob of wasabi at dinner. Do something to earn your keep.

Lesson Packages

I don't charge by the hour for lessons because it makes it too easy for students to jump in and jump out. I tailor my lesson packages to mimic a health club membership, reverse mortgage, or fractional vacation home ownership. The goal is for me to collect a large sum upfront, while locking my students into a confusing long-term commitment that has no discernible beginning, end, or clear exit strategy. Even I don't really understand it.

What Are You Hitting?

When you announce a provisional, keep it vague. Such as, "My first ball was a Molitor four. This is also a Molitor four, but this one is a little more sun faded."

My Favorite Things

I'VE BEEN IN GOLF a long time, so it should be no surprise that there are parts of the game that drive me nuts, like dealing with members, the drudgery of running junior camps, and having to explain to my General Manager why the register never balances. But there's still plenty about the game that I love. Maybe I'm getting soft as I get older, or maybe I'm just in a good mood because our hottest member here at the club, Shelby Clayman, just told one of our bag boys that her husband Barry, just left for a three-day business trip to Omaha. At any rate, while I'm sitting here during a shift change at Bottoms Up, I'm just gonna write this down on a cocktail napkin—my favorite things about the game of golf. Here goes nothing!

- Balls that kick back in play
- Downhill, downwind tee balls
- "That's good."
- Reversible belts (one side has got to be white though!)
- Net birdies
- Having a wide open look at the green from the wrong fairway
- Arnold Palmer (the golfer)

- John Daly (the drink)
- Bombing one in front of the beverage-cart girl
- Chunked chips that run out farther than you deserve
- An opponent lipping out
- "Pick it up."
- The Perfect Club
- Equitable stroke control
- Morning dumps in the ladies' locker room
- Telling blind dates that I'm a single digit
- The feel of a flushed punch out
- Short par-3s
- Drivable par-4s
- Reachable par-5s
- An opponent hitting one OB
- "Good, Good?"
- Hitting an absolute laser off the range picker
- Putting on a stripe show at Top Golf
- A bladed chip that hits the pin square
- A perfect lie in the rough
- The group ahead quitting after nine
- Lateral stakes
- The new double-hit rule
- Those girls who do pre-round back massages at fancy member/guest tournaments
- The sound of metal spikes on concrete
- Fleecing guys with vanity handicaps
- Toe hooks that run forever
- Playing up a box

Work Harder, or Don't

I TELL ALL ASPIRING tour players who come see me for advice the same thing. Somewhere out there, someone is working harder than you, but don't let it bother you, because neither one of you are good enough to make it.

Putt Better Fast!

TO PUTT WELL UNDER pressure, you must learn how to practice under pressure. I like to create little games that have meaningful outcomes. For instance, I'll place six balls around the cup roughly two feet from the hole. If I don't make all six in a row, I force myself to do something awful, like donating blood or something. Trust me, you can really feel your heart beating on those last two putts. If you can hole putts when it matters in practice, you'll be able to do it in competition.

Charity Scrambles

For my money, the four-man charity scramble is the purest form of golf. The reason is simple: it's the way the game was meant to be played. No other format is better at identifying who wants to win more. To come out on top, a scramble team must be willing to do anything in the name of victory. If you want to win your next corporate or charity scramble, I can help, but if you have even the slightest moral hesitation about a win-at-all-cost strategy, you can stop reading right now.

First things first: for your team to win, you have to understand that for those seven-plus hours on the course, the rules of golf do not apply to you. Your entire group must be 100-percent on board with this "anything goes" attitude and commit to forgetting every moral lesson your parents and teachers ever taught you and collectively go to a dark place in pursuit of a common goal: pro shop credit.

Now sometimes you might find yourself on a team that has one guy with a stick up his ass who wants to "play it straight." Fuck that guy. Although peer pressure can sometimes be effective, the best way to handle him is to get him wasted and keep him away from the scorecard. Luckily, most charity and corporate scrambles are booze-fests, and to maximize your chance of winning (and get the most of the event), everyone in your group should drink every free drink they can.

Don't worry about the hooch affecting your team's performance; your actual score and the score you post are two entirely different things. Plus, the blurrier things are for your team, the better it is for your scorecard.

This might be a good time to mention mulligans. Never purchase mulligans. Full Stop. They are a complete rip off. Go ahead and use the maximum amount of mulligans you "could" have bought, plus however many more you need.

Most scramble teams have what I like to call "dead weight." You can recognize that guy immediately. He's wearing cargo shorts, hits a Nike Sasquatch 5-wood off the tee and, for some unknown reason, uses one of those "hood covers" on his bag between rounds. According to the "rules," you'll be required to use two of his drives during the round, but you're going to treat that as more of a recommendation than a regulation. By the end of this marathon, no one will remember whose drives you used on any of the holes. It's more important to keep your eyes on the prize.

No matter what happens, you have to remember one thing: everyone is cheating. It's part of the fun of this format. Kind of like doing your taxes; we're just being creative to get the best score possible. Constantly reminding yourself of this will ease the pangs of guilt you'll undoubtedly feel when you're peacocking around the buffet before the post-round awards ceremony.

When it comes to knowing what number to post, here's a good rule of thumb: Take the lowest possible score you think any team in the event could shoot in their wildest dreams and then subtract six strokes. For example, say you're playing a par-72 course with four par-5s and a drivable par or two. The absolute lowest score a team should have the balls to post is probably 21 under par. Knowing that, you're gonna need to post a score of 45, or 27 under par. You heard me right. If this seems too low for you, then maybe you don't have the gonads for these types of events.

At any rate, if you want to win $400 in shop credit split four ways, you need to learn how to go dark and low.

The Small Pocket

WHY IS THERE a smaller version of a pocket sewn inside of my regular pocket? Has anyone else noticed this? Every time I try to get a tee, or a repair tool, or a ball marker out of my Dockers it seems to get wedged within this smaller pocket that has no business being there. Who is the dumb fuck that invented this? Show yourself!

How to Practice

THERE ARE ONLY two ways to get better at this game. The first way is to fully embrace cheating. I'm talking about noodling your ball in a bunker, miraculously "finding" your tee shot in the gunch, or my personal "go-to" move, marking your ball on the green six inches closer to the hole on every putt. The other, less desirable way to get better is hard work, dedication and practice. The former guarantees results, the latter, not so much, but if you're willing to give it a try, here's how you should go about it:

1. **Pound Drivers** - The tee ball is the most important part of the game, and the only way to get good at it is to start every practice session by hammering a monster bucket with the big stick. Really try to work up a lather. Don't get overly concerned about "where" the ball goes, this is just practice. I want you to focus on how "far" the ball goes. The modern game is all about length.

2. **Easy on the Iron Play** - After you've become physically exhausted, it's time to move on to irons. Truth be told, I rarely waste time working on my iron game because I'm a student of analytics. Ask yourself, how many times do you hit a 7-iron on the course? Maybe twice? You hit your driver 14-22 times a round (including provisionals), that's more than any other club except the putter. Any time spent doing something other than hitting the big dog is a waste in my opinion.

3. **Punch Outs** - Next it's time for my bread and butter—of course I'm talking about punch-out shots. Those of you who followed my career closely on the Mexican Mini-Tour know that I led the tour in Strokes Gained: Punching Out Sideways (SGPOS) in nine of the 14 years I was on tour. These are tough, unpredictable shots that I knew I'd have to hit eight to 12 times per round, but I

always came at them with confidence, because I'd already put in the work. The key is to find a wooded area near the range and go through every possible scenario: hard-pan, deep rough, waist-high brush, ball up against tree, left-handed because it's the only option, ball "floating" in branches of a thicket. I practiced them all, because I saw them all. When you have the confidence of knowing your punch-out game is elite, you honestly don't care where your driver goes.

4. **Chipping -** Stop making chips and pitches harder than they need to be. Focus on one shot and one club and make that your go-to. For me, it's a 64-degree wedge, wide-open, full-swing, flop-shot. I'd hit anywhere from 20-30 of these shots or as many as I could before being asked to leave the chipping area, because I'd dangerously bladed too many balls into other common areas.

5. **Putting -** Always start with lag putting in order to develop some feel. I'd grab six to eight balls and go to the far end of the practice green and pick out a hole at the opposite edge that would leave the longest putt and interfere with as many other players as possible. Then I picture an imaginary circle around the cup roughly the size of a large

hot tub and try to lag my putts into that circle. I'd hit a bunch of these until I got bored.

Playing under the Influence

IT'S JUST A RANDOM observation, but I feel like recreational golf has changed a lot in the last decade or so. I don't know if people are trying to unwind, calm their nerves or just want to get blitzed, but more and more golfers are getting absolutely shit-faced on the course. It's gotten so bad at our club that my Head Marshal Darrel Bevins and his Deputy Carl Brubaker are now required to wear body cams due to the number of drunken altercations they encounter on any given weekend. I know everyone's on edge nowadays, but you're supposed to be relaxing on the golf course; not getting blackout drunk. However, if you're one of those guys who needs a chemical alteration in order to play well, you've come to the right place, because I've done it all.

Alcohol - Some things just go together, like booze and golf. There's nothing like a 12-pack of swing lubricant to help you enjoy a round. Beer is great for a long day on the links—the calories in there keep your energy up and thanks to golf's universal "pee wherever you want" policy, you won't slow down play with frequent bathroom breaks. I think Zimas—or the kids with their hard seltzer—are better for a hot day. If you're in an event where you have to post a score and have nerve issues, I strongly suggest clear liquor. You'll get wasted faster and it won't slow you down like the brown stuff.

Weed - I used to love getting stoned while playing golf, especially when I was on tour. It calmed my nerves and made me feel more focused. The only downside was some of the spaciness, which bit me in the ass on more than one occasion. There was the time I inexplicably gave away all of my golf balls to some fans by the fourth hole and had to withdraw. Or the time I noticed a cloud formation that looked so much like Mount Rushmore that I felt physically compelled to walk off the course to tell as many people as possible about it.

There were several occasions when I got so high I forgot my score (scoring beads are your friends, stoners). Then there was the final hole of the 1994 Juarez Masters. I was right on the cut line and left myself a ten-footer on the 18th hole to play the weekend. I knew where I stood and my nerves were racing, so I took a massive toke as I walked up the fairway. On the green I stalked the putt from every angle, picked my line and stood over the putt, determined not to pull the trigger until I was sure it was going in. I drained it and I was pumped. The buzz didn't last long, though. In the scoring tent I learned that I was so high I stood over the putt for a full 13 minutes before hitting it. I got a one-stroke slow-play penalty and missed the cut. It was an absolute chickenshit call, but I'll save my disdain for rules officials for another book.

Hallucinogens - Hallucinogens and golf don't mix unless you want to have a deep conversation with your putter about why you're struggling to make the short ones (don't ask). However, when I was playing in Mexico I frequently experimented with shrooms, peyote, and ayahuasca off the course, hoping to harness my untapped inner game. It didn't work. A good example of this would be in 1996, when I totally lost my bunker game. I led the tour that season in bunkers hit and had a disastrous three-percent sand-save percentage. I needed a fix, so I embarked on a psilocybin "trip" into the Chihuahuan Desert armed with my Alien wedge, a six-pack of Mexican Coca-Cola and a sleeve of Top Flight Magnas determined to figure it out. I shit you not, when "the lights came back on" three days later I was face down in a bunker at Laredo Country Club muttering, "Daddy says use the bounce, daddy says use the bounce," over and over. Full disclosure, I did successfully convert two of 15 sand-save opportunities the following week.

Hard Narcotics - If you're serious about your game with the ultimate goal of trying to make it on Tour, I wouldn't recommend doing hard-core drugs. Not because they're not great, but because over the long haul, they're just way too expensive. When you add up the cost of travel, hotels, meals, trainers, coaches, etc., a $12,000/week cocaine habit is extremely difficult to justify. Unless you are a very top player with lucrative endorsement deals or a player getting financially backed by multimillionaires, I'd pretty much avoid the devil's dandruff on the golf course.

In closing, the irony of all this is that your favorite PGA Tour player is almost surely an absolute pill head. They kick off their day with an Adderall in their coffee to jumpstart their practice sesh, crush up some Klonopin in their PB&J to fight the nerves of grinding out five-footers, followed by a Viagra with a groupie at night and finally, an Ambien to get to sleep.

Point is, not using pharmaceuticals to help your golf game in this day and age is no different from someone trying to qualify for the U.S. Open using persimmons woods and a balata—completely stupid.

Strategy

LATE IN A MATCH, calling a petty rules infraction on your opponent is far easier and just as effective as making a birdie.

Thanks, but No Thanks

I'VE NEVER BEEN a fan of houses on the golf course.

As a homeowner you have to constantly deal with wayward golf balls bouncing off your roof and as a golfer I have to look at that dilapidated trampoline you still have in your backyard.

My Ten Bucket-List Golf Courses

As a former tour player, I've been blessed to have the opportunity to play some amazing golf courses throughout my career. From courses with oil greens on the Oklahoma Panhandle Tour to *cinco estrella* (five-star) golf courses in Mexico. I've seen it all, but there are still plenty of tracks on my bucket list that I'd love to take a crack at.

10. Shamrock Hills Golf Club, Lee's Summit, Missouri. You never forget your first! I won my first ever net championship here, just before I turned pro. I shot net 57-53-55 beating the field by 41 strokes and winning $25 in shop credit. I was immediately banned for life from the course, but I'd love to play there one more time before I die.

9. Tour 18 in Dallas, Texas. Save yourself the cost and effort of flying all over the place trying to play the world's greatest golf courses. This course has replicas of golf's most famous 18-holes all in one convenient location. Spend the money you'll save on travel to visit one of the world's true wonders; the giant big screen TV at Cowboys Stadium.

8. **Matamoros Country Club, Matamoros, Mexico.** Home to El Chapo's Taint, where my legendary eight-hole par streak came to an end. This place is always going to be near to my heart.

7. **Payne's Valley, Branson, Missouri.** Growing up in Missouri, Payne Stewart was a huge inspiration for junior golfers like me. I'd love to play here as an honor to him. Plus, it's just minutes from my timeshare.

6. **Bandon Dunes, Somewhere in Oregon.** I don't really know jack shit about it, but if I don't include this on my list, I'll be cancelled. Not today wokesters!

5. **St. Andrews, England.** Call me a traditionalist, but I'd love to take a crack at that old bitch!

4. **Top Golf, Las Vegas, Nevada.** This isn't technically a golf course, but there is so much hot ass running through that place it's making my list!

3. **Augusta National Golf Club, Augusta, Georgia.** I love watching the Masters on TV and it would be great to hit all the same shots that legends like Reed, Zoeller and Willet had to hit.

I think I'd probably light the place up too - you can't make the greens fast enough for elite players like yours truly.

2. **Pebble Beach Golf Links, Pebble Beach, California.** This is an easy one. While the views are supposed to be incredible, this is more of a financial decision. There are a bunch of widows at my club who already paid me big money to scatter their husband's ashes all over that place. I already told them I've done it and the money is long gone, but for legal reasons it would be prudent to finally deliver.

1. **Three Jack National, Kansas City, Missouri.** No surprise here. As I write this, the course is not yet completed, but I can assure you this Hank Jones signature design will be the top semi-private club in the entire Midwest.

Using Analytics to Improve Your Putting

People who have followed my career closely know that I'm a big believer in golf analytics. To me, using data and statistics to gain an edge on the competition is essential. Nowhere is this more evident than when you mark your ball on the green.

According to Shotlink data, the average 15-handicap has a .00004 percent better chance of making a 19-foot, 10-inch putt than he does a 20-foot putt. Armed with this knowledge, it only makes sense to try and gain at least an inch of hole proximity when you place your mark behind your ball and then gain another inch when you replace your ball. Purchasing a new putter, taking a lesson, or even practicing your stroke can all contribute to better results on the green, but gaining a couple inches on every putt you hit is probably the easiest way to see immediate improvement.

Better Short than Weak

IF YOU AVERAGE 220-yards off the tee with a driver and find yourself on a 220-yard, par-3, hit your hybrid, because hitting driver on a par-3 is a universal sign of weakness.

Which Tee Box is Right for You?

THERE'S A LOT OF griping in the world of golf about which tees everyone should play from. For some it's about pace of play and for others it's all about making the course "fun" and playable for everyone. For me it's simple, there are three tee boxes for three types of golfers.

First of all, tees should be red, white, and blue. I don't know how various golf courses continue to screw this one up! There's nothing more annoying than when a golf course gets cute with the colors or has some bullshit naming gimmick attached to them.

I have no idea what the "Sorenstam" tees are, or the "Screaming Eagle" tees, or the "Ian Baker Finch" tees.

I once played a course in Arizona where the starter asked me if I wanted to take on the "maroon" tees today? I said, "what are the maroon tees?" He said, "you know...the Stan Utley tees." How the fuck am I supposed to know? Stan had a pretty unremarkable career, so does that mean they are the middle tees? Or did Stan design the course and they think they have to kiss his ass by making them the super-far-back championship tees? Jesus Christ, people! Let's just keep it simple with red, white, and blue.

Now that I've cleared that up the rest is easy.

Ladies, the red tees are for you. Full stop. No, I'm not going to call them the "forward" tees or the "up" tees in a lame effort to be politically correct. I've been in the golf business for over 30 years and I can't remember one instance where a female didn't play the ladies' tees. If Natalie Gulbis ever visits your club and wants to play the "Emerald Tees" or the "Jerry Kelly" tees that's fine with me, but I don't think a rare instance like that merits a universal name change. And no, I'm not being sexist, ladies' tees are about reserving a place for women in the game by giving them their own piece of real estate.

The blue tees are for professionals. We've earned it. Speaking as someone who routinely plays the "tips," there's no better feeling than leaving the rest of the group behind and walking to the back box. I love the thought of players from several fairways over seeing me standing alone, getting ready to take on a 500-yard, plus par-5.

The white tees are for that rag-tag group of everyone who happens to be left over. High-handicaps, juniors, seniors, hacks, you name it.

So to recap:

Are you a female? Red tees.

Does your profession REQUIRE you to wear pants in order to play golf? Blue tees.

Everyone else, white tees.

Gripping the Club

IN MY OPINION golfers waste more time messing with their grip than any other part of their game. How your hands grip the club doesn't matter. Think about it. Do you worry about how many knuckles you can see when you're holding a remote control? When you eat a hot dog, do you worry where the "V" on your right hand is pointed? When you use a pen, do you tell yourself to grip it like you're holding a baby bird? Of course not, and it doesn't stop you from doing any of those things without issue!

Just grab the club any which way you want and focus your attention on something much more important, like whether you're inhaling or exhaling at impact.

The Secret of the Golf Swing— I've Figured It Out!!!

I RECENTLY FOUND an old scorecard, and on the back of it I wrote, "The Secret of Golf - I Figured It Out!!!" Below that title I scratched down the words, "right elbow like Chi-Chi, left knee goes doe-si-doe, right glute solid and away we go!" That's it. I was drinking a lot at the time that I wrote it, so I have no idea what it means, but if you can figure it out let me know.

The Pre-Shot Routine

WHEN IT COMES TO GOLF, there are a few things I'm sure of: the golf ball can never go far enough; Michelle Wie is criminally overrated; and most golfers will never improve, no matter what they do. That said, it's possible that a solid pre-shot routine can help some of you select better targets and hit more consistent shots.

When I was playing some of my best golf south of the border, I consistently employed a simple, pre-shot routine and I thought it may be able to help you shoot lower scores. It probably won't, but fuck it.

Yardage - I like to triple source my yardage, so I use a laser and then walk it off from two different yardage markers before EVERY shot. Don't worry about pace of play, we're trying to shoot a low score, not set speed records.

Conditions - I'm an information junkie, so give it all to me—humidity, wind speed, air pressure—the more, the better. I want all that data rattling around in my head before, after, and during my shot so I can make adjustments in real time.

Target - When it comes to picking a target, don't get too specific. I prefer a general area like, "the right side of the fairway," "there-ish," or "the green."

Club Selection - I'm a big fan of taking plenty of extra club and it usually pays off. In 1995, I led the Mexican Mini Tour in "greens hit on chunked shots."

Practice Swings - The first practice swing helps get the blood flowing. Don't worry about too many swing thoughts yet, you'll have time for that once you start your actual backswing.

Deep Breaths - Take a couple deep breaths to calm your mind. The only thing you should be thinking about right now is worst-case scenario outcomes.

Second Set of Practice Swings - These should be MAX EFFORT. Start imagining the shot and try to integrate your "don't" list into the swing.

Double-Check Club Selection - You'd be surprised how many times in competition I hit a 5-iron thinking it was something like an 8-iron.

Run An "Internal Checklist" - Ask, how is my body feeling at this very moment? What's at stake with this swing? Are Plan B pills 100 percent effective? Address these lingering thoughts and resolve them BEFORE swinging. It will ease the tension during the swing.

Waggle - Like offset on a golf club, I really don't know what the waggle does, but I'm a big waggle guy.

Begin Swing Thought Sequencing - If you use my proprietary 747 Swing Thought System® this is old hat to you, but any successful golf shot is powered by an exact sequence of physical actions facilitated by a series of focused, conscious thoughts. The whole, "see the ball, hit the ball" thing is bullshit.

Waggle - Love my waggles.

Last Minute Listen - Try to be aware of distant noises, such as a car door slamming, a golf cart being put in reverse, or the clank of one of your playing partners putting a club back into their bag. You'll want to frustratingly refer to one of these if you hit a shitty shot.

Pull The Trigger - Your swing thoughts and "don't" list should be firing at 100 miles-per-hour when your backswing starts. You've done the work, now's the time for your mind and body to take over. You got this!

Save It for When It Counts

I never played well in charity events, because there was rarely an incentive. I shoot a great round and some kid on dialysis gets all the money? No thanks.

Travel on Tour

The comfort and ease with which modern players are able to travel has changed so much since the days when I was on tour. Today's young players don't realize that before the advent of the internet, guys like me were forced to pay $15.99 for an adult movie in a hotel room. Granted, you could buy the more economical "24-hour" porn package for $39.99, but there was usually no fast forward function on the remote. If you got stuck on a movie with a girl or girls who weren't your type, you might have to wait an hour or more to bust a nut. I'm getting off track here, but I think you get the idea, commercial lodging in those days was cost prohibitive for me.

Red Light and Green Light Pins

Whether you play golf at a high level like me or watch tournaments on TV, you've probably heard the announcers talk about certain hole locations being a "red light" or a "green light" pin.

With the possible exception of Arron Oberholser, most of these announcers are "never was" hackers who are oversimplifying the way we elite players attack a hole. But to be fair, there is a grain of truth in what they're saying. In fact, when I first turned pro I developed my own system for attacking pins based loosely on the traffic signal analogy, which I use to this day and I think it might even be able to help you.

Red Light Pin - A Red Light Pin is one that you should absolutely avoid taking direct aim. However, when you're at an elite level like I am, there aren't many pins I can't attack because there isn't a shot that I don't have in my bag. It's not unusual for me to play for months at a time without encountering a single Red Light Pin. Not only that, one of my strengths has always been that I'm not afraid to go low or go high - which is a character trait shared by most tour professionals. You can't make birdies if you're afraid of making doubles.

Flashing Red Light Pin - This is a Red Light Pin with a caveat. You start by picking a safe target on the green away from the pin, but mentally leave yourself the option to change your mind midway through your downswing. A perfect example of a Flashing Red Light Pin is a long par-3 with the hole tucked close to water. Your initial target should be the fat of the green, but if you start your downswing and feel a good pass coming on, go ahead and make a handsy, last second adjustment to attack the pin.

This goes the other way too. Perhaps you picked an overly aggressive target and decided to chicken out after you've started your sequence. You should be mentally prepared to make an instant, mid-swing adjustment and steer your ball to a safer target.

Yellow Light Pin - I also like to call this a "Fuck-It Pin." An example of this might be a heavily guarded, drivable par-4 where your odds of hitting the green are roughly 1 in 1,000. Those odds aren't in your favor but "fuck it," because eagle putts don't grow on trees.

A Yellow Light Pin is a high-risk/low-reward play and means accepting that you'll likely make a quad for the extremely unlikely chance at making an eagle. It's a classic trade-off the guys on tour make every week.

Green Light Pin - This is pretty much 99.9 percent of the approach shots I encounter. Why? Because I'm a professional and have the ability to do what we in the biz call "work" the ball, which is just another way of saying I can get it into tight windows. Plus, with my short game, I have no fear of getting short-sided. I can almost always chip it on and two putt to save bogey.

Others - There are a few other "road signs" in my repertoire, including "Wrong Way," which is when I have to punch out to an opposite fairway, "Dead End," which is the point in a round when I WD with a phantom injury to avoid posting an embarrassing score that I know will be seen online by my peers, and "No Left Turn," which I use when I'm fighting a massive hook.

Always Snip the Red Wire

My teaching philosophy is a lot like that of a bomb defuser. Either I'm right, or it's not my problem anymore.

Club Romance

As a club professional, I have what some people like to call that "it" factor. Similar to a fighter pilot or a drummer in a rock band, I have an aura that surrounds me when I'm at the course. My "it" factor has female members as well as co-workers putting me on a type of sexual pedestal. I fully recognize this and just try to keep it light and have fun, but try not to ever fall for anyone. I use a "hit it and quit it" mentality when it comes to co-workers, which has always served me well. I don't date. I don't linger. Also, I only have office romances with subordinates, because I know I'll need the leverage if things go bad. Speaking from experience, I've had many near misses at club holiday parties, happy hours, and quiet moments in the bag room where the sexual tension is so thick you could cut it with a belly putter.

While I do my best to avoid mixing business with pleasure, when it comes to the single/divorced moms at the club, it's open season. At the end of the day, it's best to just use your judgement. If it feels right, go for it. Even if it doesn't feel right, I usually still go for it. You know what the kids say...YOLO!

My 10 Rules for Punching Out Sideways

I'VE ALWAYS FELT LIKE the punch-out shot is the most important shot in golf, because getting your ball safely back in play is paramount for avoiding big numbers. That's why I practiced it so much and that's why I'm so well known for it. Many years ago I developed my "Ten Rules" for punching out sideways and they are listed below.

1. **You have to get excited.** Listen, I get it. Nobody likes hitting a tee ball forty yards dead left into the gunch. Being a great escape artist begins with having a positive mindset. I've always been a big believer that bad attitudes make for bad punch-outs. When I would make the long walk from the tee box to the ball search area near the course's outer property line, I always made it a point to start imagining the opportunities that awaited me. Will I be stymied behind a tree, wide-open, buried, plugged, unplayable, OB, lost...or worse?

There are limitless possibilities, and I think that's what makes it fun. You have an amazing opportunity to frustrate your playing competitors and wow onlookers by getting it safely back in play! Taking what others might view as a bad situation and salvaging a bogey with a high-quality punch-out, was the hallmark of my game and probably what I'm most remembered for.

2. **When my punch-out game was on...**and I mean really ON, patrons and playing competitors alike would stop what they were doing and watch my escapes. Low punches, medium trajectory, lofted wedge punch-outs over trees, it really didn't matter, the ball would almost always end up safely back in the fairway. It got to a point in my prime where my punch-out game was so good that I could almost guarantee bogey or better, no matter how far off-line my tee ball was. It wasn't uncommon for my playing competitors to sarcastically say, "nice bogey" as they watched my tee ball sail 60-yards dead left because they intuitively knew I was going to make a great escape and salvage the hole. There are big hitters and there are short game wizards, but I can honestly say for a five-to-seven-year stretch I was the best punch-out player in the game.

3. **Practice makes perfect.** I took a lot of comfort and pride in knowing that I would never find myself in a punch-out situation that I hadn't practiced before. It's called preparation. Whether it was a left handed punch-out from my knees to avoid a cactus or a belly punch-out from under an abandoned car, I was never surprised because I had seen it before in practice.

People still talk about the punch-out I made in the 1992 Yucatan Masters while laying on my back with my ball suspended in an Acalypha bush. Was that a great punch-out? Sure. What people don't realize is, I had practiced that shot hundreds of times prior to finding myself in that situation. I think that's what set me apart from my peers at that time. While they were busy dialing in their drivers and honing their short games, Ernesto and I were deep in the "bush" putting in the work that very few other players were willing to commit to.

4. **You've got to have a ball hawk as a caddie.** My caddie Ernesto was like a hunting dog. I swear that guy could find a ball anywhere. Woods, weeds, desert, jungle, water, it didn't matter. I'll never forget the 18th hole at the 1991 Los Mochis Challenge where I hit a tee ball so far right it ended up in a pile of abandoned tires in a bar-

rio adjacent to the club's swimming pond. A good four minutes into the search and after removing at least three dozen tires, Ernesto somehow found the ball resting on a hubcap from a 1971 Peugeot 304 Wagon. After an extended discussion with a rules official, I hit this great little three-quarter punch-out back in play and turned what could have been a disaster into a double-bogey to miss the cut by twelve. A good caddie can make all the difference.

5. **Respect the roots.** One of the biggest mistakes I see amateurs make when they attempt to punch-out is not taking into account the topography and ground conditions under the ball. It's paramount. People sometimes forget that they're technically off of the golf course. You have to respect the fact that you're in an area that has geology as its greenskeeper. I've seen more than my share of playing competitors sprain a wrist or injure a hand, because they didn't respect the awesome power of the Earth's surface. You have to be ready for anything—roots, rocks, stumps, appliances, hard pan, rebar, cactus—and play your shot accordingly. That's why my method of aggressively flinching just prior to impact eliminates any "surprises" at the moment of truth and cuts down on potential injuries.

6. **It's always the smallest branches that get you.** In the 1995 Soledad de Graciano Sanchez, all I needed to do was finish with a bogey on 18 to make the cut on the number and advance to match play. After blowing my tee ball dead left into a Guarombo orchard, Ernesto found my ball and set me up for a very standard "back facing the target" one-armed, flip punch out. Perhaps it was a lack of concentration or maybe it was arrogance, but I didn't even notice the thumb-size limb about five yards in front of me. Naturally, I clipped just enough of it to careen my ball into the Telmex corporate hospitality tent where I took an inadvertent illegal drop and ended up making a quad. Moral of the story, respect every branch.

7. **Never be embarrassed to putt it.** I get it, nobody wants to be seen using a putter 170-yards from the green, but the name of the game is getting the ball back in play by whatever means necessary. I see players today try to hit the sexy punch-out instead of the smart punch-out and their scorecard ends up paying the price. Even though I am most known for my aerial punches, people might be surprised to know that my first thought when I assess a situation is, can I putt it? That's why I had my tech team at RAM specially outfit my Zebra putter with seven degrees of

loft for just such occasions. It's these types of little things that gave me a leg up on my competitors when it came to punching out.

8. **Enter and exit the woods with swagger.** I made it a point to begin every ball search with extreme cockiness and arrogance. Whether it was berating a volunteer or blowing off a star struck child attempting to help me in the search, I wanted everyone to know that this was "my office" and I'm busy at work. Once the ball was found, I liked to really make an "over the top" production out of how difficult the shot was going to be. I might audibly complain about how bad the lie was or engage in a long discussion with Ernesto about how incredibly tight the window which I was attempting to go through was. This way, if I pulled the shot off I'm a heroic shot-maker and if I don't, at least I get credit for attempting the near impossible.

9. **Never take an unplayable.** Listen, I'm the first to acknowledge that it's possible to get in some pretty tough spots off the tee, but I would always do everything in my power to avoid taking a penalty. You have to remember, my fans didn't come out and spend their hard earned dinero to watch me take drops. They came to see an ab-

solute punch-out clinic and I wasn't about to let them down. Did this get me in trouble on occasion? Sure. However, the looks of wonderment on a young fan's face as I whistled a little hold off 6-iron straight sideways to the safety of the fairway made it all worthwhile.

10. **When things go south, rapid fire.** Every once in a while you'll get into a situation where your first punch-out attempt can put you in an even worse position. Whether it's a bad-luck ricochet, a whiff, or an embedded ball that gets embedded even deeper. This is not a time to "reset" and patiently go through a long drawn out process of evaluating your next shot to minimize the damage that has clearly already been done. It's time for rapid fire. The reality is that you had one chance to get out of trouble to save the hole and you blew it. At this point you'll be doing your playing partners and everyone else a favor by just taking indiscriminate rapid hacks at the ball until you finally escape trouble.

Advice I Hope You Never Have to Use

Trust me, I've seen some shit. Don't ask me how I know this, but if you're ever in a position where a cartel enforcer is going to break one or more of your fingers but lets you pick which one, as a golfer go with the left, ring finger first; followed by left, middle finger; right, middle finger; right, index finger; and right pinkie (but only if you overlap.) If you're a lefty just go with the opposite of this list. Also, never bet on "professional" Guatemalan soccer.

Being a Teacher

A few years back, one of the kids I was teaching advanced to the finals of our local city championship, setting up a showdown with the number-one junior player in the state. The night before the match the kid was nervous as hell and called me for a few words of wisdom. After I established that I considered the call a paid lesson and would need to charge him, I agreed to give him some advice. Frankly, I didn't think this kid was that good, so my first thought was that it was a miracle he'd made it that far, so I didn't know exactly what to say to him.

To make matters worse, he caught me eight Zimas deep into a nice little Chili's happy hour sesh. Chili's is a safe space for me and I wasn't prepared to deal with the first world problems of some member's kid. For that, I have to get in the zone. When I pull into the parking lot at work, I sit in my Miata for a few moments before getting out to prepare myself for the onslaught of bullshit that comes from dealing with my members. I pause and whisper a little daily aspiration to myself, something like, "this beats selling mobile phones," or "do it for your timeshare in Branson," or "it could be worse, you could be caddieing for Matt Kuchar." After that's out of the way I'm able to withstand all the members' inane bullshit, like hearing a hole-by-hole recap of their round, or complaints about our temporary greens or questions about an off-color remark I made in the club newsletter.

Anyway, since I was fully unplugged and blowing off some steam, this kid's call caught me off guard. After taking a beat, the only thing that came to mind was, "your mom is half Korean, so there's always a chance." I thought it was genius advice, but it didn't really land with the kid and he pressed me some more. He asked me, "do you think I can win tomorrow?" At that point I didn't know what else to say, so I told him I was driving into a canyon and about to lose reception and hung up on him.

A few days later I ran into his dad at the driving range. I tried not to make eye contact, but he chased me down and caught up to me in the back of the cart barn. With a finger in my face, he informed me that his son had lost his match 8 & 7 and was completely unprepared, thanks to my incompetence. As he stormed out, he violently kicked over a massive stack of empty range ball buckets and screamed that his wife was Native American, not Korean.

The moral of the story is that teaching golf is hard. Advice that works for one student may not work for another. If I had it to do all over again, I would probably have forwarded the kid a few random David Leadbetter videos off of YouTube and called it a day. In the world of elite golf instruction, sometimes you have to make split second decisions and just live with the results.

The Dewsweepers

THEY WAKE UP at 4:15 a.m. and head to the course. The predawn darkness surrounds them as they sit in their car and wait for the first signs of life in the pro shop. Some call them the "rabbits" or the "Dawn Patrol," but most refer to them as "The Dewsweepers." These are the grey-haired, knee-braced, Skechers-wearing cheapskates who play 18-holes before you've even felt the first contraction from your morning dump. As a club pro, I see these guys as a blessing and a curse. They're as low maintenance as it gets, but annoying as they come, and I hear their pushcarts full of rattling clubs in my nightmares.

Fast play is their best and perhaps only positive attribute, sort of. Sure, it's great that they play quick, but they're out-of-sight before the sun comes up. Are you really setting the pace of play if you're making the turn while the day's second group is still hitting the snooze button?

Their obsession with fast play is eclipsed only by their cheapness. I did the math at my club. After the Groupon and the Super Seniors annual pass discounts, they're paying about $1.50 per round. And good luck getting them to spend anything on food and beverage. These guys wouldn't buy a Snickers bar even if our beverage cart girl Anastasia offered a free hand job with it. The only thing they appreciate more than the Summer Solstice is discovering a small mistake in their favor on their monthly club bill.

They live by a creed that says new golf balls are for suckers, paying a cart fee is an abomination, and getting home by 9 a.m. to mow the yard is the greatest thing in the world.

So True

Don't swing your swing; your swing is terrible. Try to swing Louis Oosthuizen's swing; it's so much better than yours.

On-Course Bathroom Strategy

VERY FEW GOLF PROS have the self-confidence to talk about this publicly, but having a bathroom strategy before teeing off can make or break your round. I've always been amazed at how many otherwise, very smart people will meticulously plan for some things in life, like retirement or their children's education, yet willy-nilly head to the first tee without giving ANY thought whatsoever to the ramifications of shitting their pants mid-round. This is an issue that's close to my heart, primarily because my guts are an absolute dumpster fire, and even on a good day, I experience a lot of loose stools. Early in my playing career I blamed it on the challenges of mini-tour life, like sleeping in my car, living off roadside "carne asada," and the white hot pressure of playing professional golf for a paycheck. Now that I'm a club pro, I have to deal with the stress that comes with serving the general public coupled with eating at Chili's for dinner on a near nightly basis. The quality of the food is top notch, but rich, hence my never-ending battle with the gout.

When it comes to spending half your day outside, hundreds of yards from a bathroom, don't be a victim. Follow these easy tips for staying clean and comfortable in your next round.

1. **Leave yourself time** to take a crap before you tee off, including time to finish ALL of your business. There's often a second round lying in wait.

2. **Know the location** of all the on-course bathrooms before you peg it, and confirm with the marshal or pro shop that they're operational and unlocked. Trust me, you don't want to race to a bathroom only to soil yourself by hitting a locked door at the finish line. That's how you ruin a nice pair of Dockers.

3. **ALWAYS use** the women's restroom. Trust me, there's never anyone in there and you will thank me later.

4. **Take a cart** so if you're in a really bad way you can get to the crapper ASAP.

5. **If you have a blowout** and need to clean up, sacrifice the underwear first, golf towel second, socks and/or golf glove third, and knit head covers as a last resort. Don't forget to bury the evidence.

That's it. Oh, and when it comes to peeing on the golf course, just let loose anywhere. Doesn't matter. It's one of the little things that makes our game so great!

Odd Jobs

During some of my more lean years on tour I would make ends meet by running drugs back and forth from Juarez to El Paso. I got really good at it and found myself doing it all the time. In fact, my handler used to joke that because my anus had become so enlarged, stuffing an eight-ball of coke up my ass reminded him of throwing an unopened bag of flour down a hallway.

It was great money for a side gig, but I'm not sure if it was worth it. The Sinaloa Cartel ended up putting out a Fatwa on me that still stands to this day.

The Business of Golf

I AM NOT NAIVE, BUT it took me a while to learn that for guys at my level, golf is a business. I understand that there are times when sponsors decide to go in a different direction.

What I don't understand is the very public way in which many of these splits happen. I had a near 20-year relationship with Lynx Golf snuffed out in a single tweet and was defamed by the company online. I felt disrespected, but also, I felt like they were hurting themselves. Who sold more Crystal Cat Chippers, Fred Couples or me? I got a $5 spiff for every one I moved. Freddy didn't have that kind of incentive.

I had hoped the split would be amicable, like my first and third divorce, but to add insult to injury, Lynx wouldn't buy back my Black Cat irons. Totally classless move on their part. Sure, it didn't help that their field rep filed a credible sexual harassment suit against me, but in my defense, she was so hot she had no business calling on golf pros. I don't make the rules.

My deal with U.S. Kids Golf was even worse. The fine print in my contract required me to play their actual equipment in competition. I gamed a 34-

inch driver for almost two years. It probably ruined my career. Luckily, most of the kids on tour now-a-days have agents with college degrees, so some of the stuff that happened to me can be avoided, but the business of golf can be brutal.

Leave the Dockers at Home

WHILE I'VE FORGOTTEN more about golf than most of you will ever know, my knowledge goes beyond the course. One of my areas of expertise is my passion as a strip club connoisseur. As a whole, the amateurish behavior I see at the clubs is embarrassing, but there's something I just can't let slide any longer. Nothing gets me more pissed than seeing a group of guys walk into a strip club and all of them are wearing jeans or Dockers. This is a massive fail. When getting dressed for the strip club, your outfit starts and finishes with your pants. You want as little fabric between your junk and the dancer as possible.

Before your next visit to the strip club, head to your local Ross and pick out the flimsiest, lightest pair of pants you can find. Track pants work great... so do cheap sweats. Basically anything you would play pick-up basketball in. Hold them up to the light, can you see through the material? Good. The thinner the fabric, the sweeter the lap dance. Thank me later.

Five Things Parents of Young Golfers Should Know

As a parent, there's nothing you want more in life than to raise the next Tiger Woods or Brooks Koepka. Or if you have daughters, the next HeeJeong Lim or Ji Yeong Kim. The problem is, achieving this takes not only a huge commitment on the kids part, but on yours as well. Keep things simple by following my five tips for raising an elite junior player.

1. **Get Them Started Early** - Tiger Woods was on the Mike Douglas Show when he was 27 months old. Let that sink in for a minute. While your son is probably still doing number twos in the bathtub, Tiger was showing Bob Hope and Jimmy Stewart how to hit a tight draw on national television. My point is that no matter how old your kid is, it's probably already too late.

2. **Stick to Golf** - Letting your kid engage in any activity other than golf should be strictly forbidden. I could be wrong, but I don't remember Dustin Johnson wasting his time playing fucking soccer.

Keep your eyes on the prize. Besides, if they're gonna get burn-out and depression you would rather it happen at age eight, not 18, right?

3. **Make It All About the Money -** If your daughter is going to be an elite player, she needs the best of everything—equipment, private club access, lessons, apparel, training aids, you name it. Naturally, you'll need to provide all of this but while doing so, constantly give her subtle guilt trips on how much all this stuff costs because that little bit of added pressure might be the difference between a Division 1 scholarship and her hating you forever.

4. **Trophies or Bust -** At this age, there's no such thing as playing for the love of the game. It's about winning at all costs. PGA Tour player Sean O'Hair's father famously took a lot of heat for being tough on his son, but it produced a kid who's made $25 million (and counting) on tour. Who's the bad parent now?

5. **Treat It Like a Job -** There will be plenty of time for fun when they get to a Top 10 world ranking and are sending you and your wife $50,000/month stipends. Until then, let's keep this all business. It's school and golf. Period. And not necessarily in that order.

(Miss It, Miss It, Miss It)

HOPING YOUR competitors play poorly is every bit as important as hoping that you play well.

Augusta National and the Masters

I HAVE A LOVE/HATE relationship with Augusta National.

When I was a brash young pro on the Mexican Mini-Tour, I used to tell people that even if I was invited by a member, I wouldn't go play Augusta until I EARNED my way into the Masters. At that time I was breaking 80 almost on-demand, and I instinctively knew that if given the chance, nobody would be able to punch out of those Georgia pines better than I could. Sadly, partly due to performance and partly due to politics, I was never able to qualify. Now that I'm well into my 40s, absent a major breakthrough with my short game, I doubt if I ever will. Complicating matters even more, Augusta threatened to sue me when I tried to sell my popular Yucatan Masters merchandise on my website. Never mind that Yucatan National and the Yucatan Masters pre-date the event, which we all recognize as golf's first "major" of the year.

The long story short is, like you, I've never had the opportunity to step foot on the grounds of Augusta National. However, a few years ago I had an amazing opportunity to sit down and interview someone who has. Mr. Randy Beck. Randy was a Groupon member at our club, who also happened to work as an Apprentice Plumber at KC Snake-n-Rooter Plumbing. Randy got the opportunity of a lifetime when Trevor Hampton, a regional sales manager for a PVC pipe company, scored two badges to a coveted Tuesday practice round at the 2016 Masters—won by Danny Willet.

Even though Randy has since been kicked out of our club for stealing range balls, this interview stands the test of time, because it literally pulls back the curtain on one of the most famous golf courses in the world, so sit back, relax, and let Randy take you inside the forbidden world of Augusta National Golf Club.

CPG: Tell us what it's like as you're at the gate waiting to get in?

Randy: All I remember was it was very early in the morning. Trevor was obsessed with being one of the first people in line and I was obsessed with getting shit-faced. I knew draft beers at the Masters were only like a dollar each, but I wasn't taking any chances, so I had several pockets of my cargo shorts filled with mini bottles of Fireball.

Trevor was super nervous for some reason. He was constantly telling me how "serious" this was and to watch what I do and say. Unlike myself, Trevor was dressed to impress. He went with an oversized FootJoy polo shirt (pink) buttoned all the way up, khaki shorts (no belt) and black Oakley golf shoes with white footy socks.

When they opened the gate, I immediately took off running because I wanted to be first in line at the merch tent to buy a set of shot glasses, but one of the guys in the green coats shouted that I wasn't allowed to run, but I never looked back and kept going. What I didn't realize was that since they couldn't catch me, they detained Trevor and escorted him off the property. He ended up watching "Live From" on the Golf Channel for the next eight hours in a nearby Little Caesars Pizza restaurant. He was literally inside the gates for less than 30 seconds.

CPG: OK. You got your shot glasses and you headed over to the first tee. Tell us what the players will be facing on hole number one?

Randy: They're facing an easy par. Period. Granted, I'm pretty long for a 12-handicap but when I stood on that tee I figured if I nutted one I could get it just past the fairway bunker, which would leave me anywhere from a 9-iron to a gap wedge in (and these guys are as long or longer than I am). So this is a pretty easy hole out of the gate that should allow these guys to ease into their round.

CPG: Ok, so an easy start. I think number two is a par-5, what's it like?

Randy: Pretty much a gimme birdie hole. It goes downhill and turns to the left. The thing I remember most about this hole is that I took a massive dump in the porta-john right next to the tee box and Brandt Snedeker's wife happened to go in right after me. I felt bad for her.

CPG: Ok, so any player worth a damn is in red numbers by now. What does number three do?

Randy: It's laughably short. Like maybe 350 yards. Honestly, at this point I'm starting to wonder what all the fuss is about. I remember thinking…is this the Masters or the ANA Inspiration? We have holes here at our club longer than that.

CPG: That's great insight, Randy. When you watch the broadcast, they constantly hype the course up to make us think it's more difficult than it is in order to add drama. I think it's a ratings ploy by the guys at CBS. Let's move on to number four. It's a long par-3…right?

Randy: This is probably the first what I would call "legit" hole on the golf course. It plays about 240 which is a hybrid for me or maybe a careered 3-iron. The thing is, the turf is so much better than what we're used to at our club. No crab grass or hard pan at all. None! So even if you miss the green, it's a pretty easy up and down. Especially for these guys.

CPG: We're halfway through the front nine, is this where Augusta starts to show its teeth?

Randy: The short answer is yes, but for one key reason. They don't have a temporary green on number five like we do here at our club, you absolutely cannot relax with an auto 2-putt. In fact, there wasn't a temp on the entire golf course that I can remember. That's why this is a major championship, you literally have to earn every shot.

CPG: Yeah, it's like Thursday Night Men's League on steroids. That's why it's such a great event. Let's keep moving. I've always felt like number six and seven are some of the lesser known holes on the golf course. Describe them for us.

Randy: Six is a throw-away par-3 and number seven is a cookie cutter par-4 that you might see on any public course in America. The only reason I remember number seven is because that's the hole where I took my shirt off to catch some rays and a security guard was there to make me put it back on before I could even tie it around my waist. It was hot that day and I sweat a lot when I drink.

CPG: I've always thought the golf course really starts to get good on number eight, this is a long par-5 that plays way uphill. Right?

Randy: (laughs) The thing people don't realize is that the course is a lot flatter than it looks on TV. But you're right, the eighth hole is extremely long and starts to work its way up to the clubhouse. As you know, I'm one of the longest guys here at our club and this would be a three-shot hole even for me, so look for all the guys to lay back to a comfortable yardage here and let their wedges do the talking.

CPG: We've seen some drama on number nine over the years. In 1992, Jay Don Blake famously made double on Friday to miss the cut by 12. What do you remember about that hole?

Randy: I think it's a par-4 but I'm not sure because that's the hole where my old lady (Trish) was blowing up my phone because she had just discovered a $1,200 charge on our CapitalOne Visa from

Magic City in Atlanta, Georgia, from the night before. She totally lost her shit about it.

CPG: They say the tournament doesn't start until the back nine on Thursday. Tell us what the players can expect on number ten?

Randy: Listen, I'm not gonna sit here and say it's "easy," but that hole is straight down hill, okay? Literally all you have to do is get something airborne and it's gonna run forever. It sets up perfect for my Srixon 2-wood because I can hit that thing a mile high. I remember Vijay and Mark O'Meara were on that tee when I walked by and I half-jokingly/half-seriously asked if I could hit one just for fun and they TOTALLY blew me off. I've never been a big Vijay fan, but I actually used to like O'Meara. He's dead to me now.

CPG: OK, we're getting into the meat of the course. Let's head to 11.

Randy: This hole is gettable if you can carry your tee ball dead straight about 320 to get over the hill. On the approach, there's water left and a big bailout area right where everyone was going. I've never seen so many cowards. Hello! This is the Masters! They don't hand green jackets out to guys who aim for collection areas. If I was playing, I would take dead aim there.

CPG: This takes us to perhaps the most famous hole on the course...the par-3 12th. Describe it for us.

Randy: (laughing) I mean, it's a 150-yard, par-3, okay? I've never been so underwhelmed in my life. I watched about four groups come through and every single guy hit the middle of the green with a carefree 9-iron or wedge. Whoever designed this course either took his eye off the ball or got lazy when this hole was put in. I saw several par-3s way harder than this on some of the Disney courses I played when Trish and I went to Orlando last summer.

CPG: So not much bite so far. Let's go to the par-5 on 13. What do you remember thinking about that hole?

Randy: The only thing I remember thinking at that point was that the little gift I left Mandy Snedeker three hours earlier might have only been an opening salvo. I decided to skip holes 13, 14 and 15 and head over to the concession area near the 16th green to get two more Miller Lites and hit the porta-john again.

CPG: OK, not a big deal, I don't remember a lot happening on those three holes over the years anyway. Let's talk about the par-3 on 16.

Randy: Well, I'd like to but I didn't get to see much of it. When I came out of the shitter, I noticed two chairs that were totally unoccupied behind the green (right about where Tiger holed that chip back in 2005). I decided to go over there and set up camp. Just as I'm taking my socks and shoes off to get comfortable, an elderly couple approaches and tells me I've taken their chairs. I immediately told them to go pound sand because they abandoned them. They then claimed there's some bullshit Masters rule that says you can leave your seats and they're always saved. Just as I was leaning back in the chair telling them Clifford Roberts himself couldn't get me to move, I was tackled by four Georgia State Troopers and two rent-a-cops and I briefly lost consciousness. The next thing I remember, I woke up in an Arby's parking lot on Washington Road just across from the entry gates.

CPG: Randy, I can't thank you enough for taking the time to sit down with me to share your experiences with my readers.

Randy: Anytime, CPG.

The 747 Swing Thought System®

IN THE WORLD OF elite golf instruction, one of the most damaging things I hear my peers teach is the idea that players can hit good golf shots by simply "being athletic." I can't think of worse advice. The golf swing is a highly complicated act, which involves over 144 different body parts, muscles and joints that all need to work in concert. This can't be accomplished by simply "being athletic." If an experienced F-18 fighter pilot handed you the controls mid-flight and told you to land on an aircraft carrier by simply "being athletic," could you do it? Of course not! You would crash into the ocean, or worse yet hit the flight deck, killing dozens of brave U.S. servicemen and women. Flying an F-18 is difficult, and so is the golf swing.

Many years ago I developed a system to simplify the golf swing. It's called the 747 Swing Thought System®. Think of it as an instruction manual for the golf swing in real time. This system involves 18 simple swing-thoughts that you must memorize, recite and execute during the shot. Seven swing-thoughts during the backswing, four swing-thoughts during the transition and seven, final swing-thoughts during the downswing. Hence 747. I am not going to explain or go into great detail on each thought; that is for another book. However, for the first time ever in print, I am going to list each and every swing thought of the 747 Swing Thought System® in order.

The Takeaway

1. Low and slow.

2. Hinge wrist 88 degrees.

3. OK, this is really happening.

4. Free time.

5. Are you sure you hinged 88 degrees? Because it felt like it could have been 70 or 75 degrees.

6. RESET.

7. Where's Waldo?

The Transition

1. "Hideki Matsuyama," "Hideki Matsuyama," "Hideki Matsuyama."

2. Right Elbow finds True North.

3. "Don't do the DJ."

4. OH SHIT, HERE WE GO.

The Downswing

1. Left elbow gets a party invite.

2. Turn and burn - (but don't under turn and don't over burn).

3. Don't go right. You always fucking go right!

4. Sit on the beach ball, but don't let it pop.

5. Look up like Duval, but not as much as Annika.

6. Get airborne.

7. FLIP IT!!!!

Glory Days

My greatest moment in golf since I retired competitively was probably the 73 I shot back in May of 2009. My second greatest moment was probably when nobody noticed I didn't post the 73 that I shot back in May of 2009.

Listening to Your Body

First-tee jitters are your body's way of telling you that you have no business playing in this golf tournament.

"What'd Ya Shoot?"

How many times have you been asked that question as you sat down in the grill room after a Saturday afternoon round or maybe walking up to a gaggle of your fellow club members standing by the scoring table at your Club Championship? It's such a simple question. It's such a direct question. It's a question that could be answered with a simple number such as 88, 91 or 96 etc. Like so many things in life, it's not quite that easy.

The reality is, what happened to you on the course today cannot adequately be described with just a number. In order to give your score the proper justice it deserves, you'll need to do more. I know it may sound counter-intuitive, but the people asking you what you shot aren't really looking for a number...they're looking for a story.

The thing that you need to recognize is that everyone but you got the most out of their round. The putts they should have made, they made. The bounces they should have gotten, they got. The ill-timed gust of wind that could have come up, never did. They didn't leave any shots out there. You, on the other hand, experienced a round filled with burned edges, lip outs and outrageous hardpan lies and people want to know about it. At least, you need them to know about it. In order to paint a more complete picture of what you shot, follow these simple tips.

1. Go in Order - Obviously you want to include everything but don't confuse your listener by starting with the fried egg on number eight, followed by the distant car alarm in your backswing on number two followed by the 360-degree lip out on number 13. Skipping around can be disorienting. Start on hole number one and move sequentially all the way to number 18.

2. Speak in Hyperbole - To drive your misfortune home, include language such as, "I have never seen a worse lie" or "you could hit a monster bucket from there and not get a worse bounce" or, "I've been a member here 12 years and have never seen a ball come to rest there." People need to know that this wasn't just run-of-the-mill bad luck. Your score today was due to generational, or perhaps even Biblical misfortune.

3. Include Gray Areas - Does being "between clubs" or having a sprinkler head in your field of vision qualify as legitimate bad breaks? Probably not, but go ahead and include them in your recap anyway.

4. **Don't Reciprocate -** Let's face it, nobody else's round is going to be as compelling as yours, so once you're finished don't burden your listener by asking them what they shot. If you sense they're starting to engage about the details of their round, quickly change the subject to your son's Little League baseball game last night in order to stay on a topic that everyone is interested in.

Real Money Players

People ask me all the time what makes a great NET player, and I think it's that innate ability to make a five net four when you absolutely have to.

Course Marshals

As a club professional at an elite semi-private facility that accepts Groupons, I wear a lot of hats. In addition to teaching the game at a high level, I also own the shop, manage beverage-cart operations and handle all aspects of outside services. It's a big job. Luckily, I've been around long enough to know that the key to any successful golf operation is surrounding myself with the right people. The right team makes my job a lot easier and more importantly, makes me look good.

For those of you familiar with my G.O.A.T. beverage-cart girl Anastasia, who I personally recruited and hired, you know that my human-resource prowess is without peer. Aside from the beverage cart girl, the most critical hire a club professional can make is the on-course marshal position. The right marshal can set the tone for the entire golf course.

How do you make the right hire? Whatever you do, ignore the temptation to select a customer-service oriented individual with a friendly disposition. That's not important. If you want to keep rounds under six hours and assure all beverages are bought on-site, you want a guy who has an "edge". You want a guy consumed with anger who literally dares members to take their cart off the path at a 70-degree angle. You want a guy who has been given authority for the first time in his life and chooses to exercise it with extreme prejudice. You want a guy willing to be the judge, jury, and executioner all in exchange for free golf. A man that patrols the golf course as if our country's national security literally depends on it, not to mention a passionate advocate of our Second Amendment. A virtual powder keg who believes the mere sight of a member hitting chip shots onto the practice putting green warrants a physical confrontation. Sound impossible to find the right guy? Check out my four tips below for vetting course marshal candidates and you'll have your members terrified in no time.

1. **Pedigree -** A retired, divorced male is a must, but don't forget to look closely at their work history. I've found that disgruntled union workers with a chip on their shoulder make great candidates. Also, be on the look out for career high school vice-principals who believe that the end of corporal punishment marked the downfall of our public education system.

2. **Examine Interests -** Heavy drinkers and NRA members are a sweet spot. I also love candidates who drive a truck fashioned with a camper shell.

3. **Criminal History** – Always do a background check, but whatever you do, don't shy away from a candidate with a rap sheet. Personally, I won't even interview a marshal candidate if he doesn't have at least one road rage conviction.

4. **Dress for Success** - My course marshal, Darrel Bevins, showed up to his first day of work in fatigues, but he's an admitted overachiever. If a candidate meets the criteria above and shows up to the interview wearing a MAGA hat and a Members Only jacket, you've probably found your man.

Golf's Toughest Shot

THE MOST DIFFICULT SHOT for any amateur golfer to pull off is the one AFTER they've just hit a great shot. Statistically speaking, their odds of nutting back-to-back shots is basically zero.

Dating Strippers

LIKE MANY FORMER professional athletes, I often find myself in relationships with strippers. This can often be a blessing as well as a curse. It's a blessing, because I love hot girls who are willing to trade sex for a brush with fame, but the inevitable clash of demanding careers is usually too much to overcome. It's just too hard to see each other enough to cultivate a relationship.

I've dated countless strippers, and while I typically work from 7 a.m. to 9 p.m. they dance from 9 p.m. to 3 a.m. That doesn't leave us with a lot of quality time to spend together. We're like two ships with Hep C passing in the night. This is the issue I ran into with my first wife, Mercedes, as well as with my second wife, Brandi. My third wife was just flat-out nuts.

The sad reality is that anyone in my line of work who excels at their craft has to be selfish with their time in order to achieve their goals. It's what makes them great. It's one of the traits I think I share with Tiger. Sex addiction being the other.

How to Win Every Rules Dispute

If you ever find yourself involved in an on-course rules dispute with a playing competitor, you have to remember two critical things. Neither you, nor the person you're having the dispute with has a fucking clue what they're talking about! The book comprising the Official Rules of Golf is a little bit like the Bible, there's lots of information in there, but nobody can comprehend a word of it.

More importantly, the loudest and boldest personality always wins. Stake out a position and never waver! The more obnoxious you are when making your argument, the more likely it is that your opponent will back down and begrudgingly defer to your opinion.

The Key to Alignment

Of all the fundamentals, alignment is the most overrated. Your subconscious knows if you aren't lined up properly and will reroute your swing accordingly. Trust it!

Pre-round Preparation

To be totally honest, there's not a lot the "average Joe" can learn from the stars on the PGA Tour. Why? They're thoroughbreds, and in no way does your sad excuse for a golf game compare to theirs. However, there is a lesson to be learned on how the pros get ready for their round. From the moment a professional golfer arrives on property every minute is meticulously planned to prepare their body and mind for peak performance.

I think amateurs should also map out their pre-round schedule to get the most out of their game. Here's an example of how you might best use your time before your next round.

- **Forty-five minutes before your tee time:** Alarm clock goes off. Hit the snooze button (allowing your body to awaken slowly and with minimal stress before your round.)
- **Thirty-five minutes before your tee time:** Assure your wife/girlfriend you'll be home in "like four hours max," and that you'll have the entire afternoon free to spend with her.
- **Thirty minutes before your tee time:** Hop into the car. OPTIONAL: spill hot coffee on your crotch to activate your nervous system—a key component to having on course presence.
- **Twenty-five minutes before your tee time:** Text one of your playing partners and tell them you're stuck in traffic and will be at least ten minutes late.
- **Fifteen minutes before your tee time:** Screech into the parking lot. Text playing partner again, this time asking him to pay for you and that you'll "get him later."
- **Ten minutes before your tee time:** IMPORTANT - Find the nearest bathroom and take a crap.
- **Five minutes before your tee time:** Buy a breakfast sandwich or hot dog.

- **Four minutes before your tee time:** Swallow food, don't waste too much time and energy on chewing.
- **Three minutes before your tee time:** Sprint to driving range. See if anyone has left a few range balls behind. If not, find a small patch of grass and blade a few chips.
- **Two minutes before your tee time:** IMPORTANT - Find the nearest bathroom and pop the clutch on another crap.
- **Tee time:** Arrive at the practice green. Drop a few balls and bang them around like you've never been on practice green before. Hit some stupidly long putts, half-heartedly stroke a few shorties, try a grip you've never practiced before - it's all good.
- **Three minutes past your tee time:** Find your golf cart/playing partners.
- **Five minutes past your tee time:** Arrive on the first tee and reference the traffic one more time.
- **Six minutes past your tee time:** IMPORTANT - Time to stretch! Don't let anyone hurry you. You paid an $80 green fee and this is your tee box now. Besides, you're going to be on the course for the next five-plus hours, what's the rush? Any stretch will do, but the louder you groan the better.

- **Eight minutes past your tee time:** Fumble through your bag for a usable golf ball or borrow one and some tees from your playing partners.
- **Ten minutes past your tee time:** Swing away!
- **Ten minutes and fifteen-seconds after your tee time:** Declare a breakfast ball and ask one of your buddies to toss you another ball.

The Most Overrated Accomplishment in Golf

IF THERE'S ONE accomplishment in golf that's completely overrated, it has to be the hole-in-one. Let's face it, there's virtually zero skill involved. It's pure luck.

I've had a handful of aces myself, but none of them were "sanctioned" because they either: A) occurred on a temporary green, B) were during a provisional shot or mulligan or C) happened while I was playing as a single. It doesn't really matter though, because I wouldn't go around bragging about them anyway. Holes-in-one are like dreams, nobody wants to hear about them.

I've always felt like a much more impressive golf stat would be the number of beverage-cart girls you've slept with. Now there's an accomplishment that takes real skill. Think about it. Would you rather hear that old member at your club drone on about his 12 career aces, or hear him give all the juicy details of the 12 beverage-cart girls he's banged? It's a no-brainer.

Hell, they could even make shadow boxes for the occasion that includes a picture of you and the cart girl along with the can of Michelob Ultra you purchased right when the flirting started. I'm just spit-balling here, but you get the idea. I think it's past time we start recognizing golfers for actual accomplishments.

My Faith

WHEN YOU PLAY this game for a living, whether at the tour level or as a club pro, I think it's critical to have what I call that "invisible caddie in the sky." Unfortunately, I'm unable to attend church, because I have to work on Sunday mornings, but my faith guides me in everything I do. Most of my prayers are associated with a given college football team covering a point spread or a member event getting rained out. Sometimes I pray for more substantial things, like for a hot mom of one of my junior player's to get divorced, or for my general manager to contract COVID, or for the Ashworth rep to somehow lose her moral compass...stuff like that.

Elevating Your Game Is Overrated

Always try to play with players who aren't as good as you, because winning today is a lot more important than getting better tomorrow.

Always Go for It

IF YOU'RE EVER IN a position to hit driver off the deck, or a backwards, over the shoulder, flop shot (ala Phil Mickelson), or a hook-around-a-tree that Bubba Watson probably wouldn't even try, ALWAYS go for it. These high-risk/high-reward shots aren't about strategy, course management or scoring, these are opportunities to do something special. Let me explain. Say you're in position to reach a par-5 in two, if you roast a driver off the deck. There's a 99.99 percent chance that you'll either top it or hit a monster slice and make a big number. The least likely result is nutting it and giving yourself a putt for eagle. So why should you consider this play? You'll likely never have an ace, win a club championship or break 90, but maybe, just maybe, if the stars align you can pull off something special on the golf course just once in your life. Always go for it.

Playing with Women

I'VE BEEN IN THIS game for nearly 40 years, and during that time one of the biggest changes I've seen is the emergence of women golfers. Once a marginalized group who were often relegated to tee times after two p.m., ladies nowadays are seen all over the golf course and I think that's great for the game.

If you play golf regularly, you need to realize there will come a day when you and your buddies show up for your Saturday morning tee time only to find that the starter has decided to round out your foursome by adding a lone woman to your group. Your first instinct might be to complain to the shop, but don't bother. In the age of the "Me Too Movement," it's no longer acceptable to openly discriminate on the basis of gender. Forcing her to wait for a threesome of ladies to show up or banishing her over to the par-3 course is no longer a viable option. My advice is to get a better attitude! Playing with a woman can still be a lot of fun. Just remember to alter your behavior slightly by following these seven simple tips.

1. **Give Her Your Bona Fides -** After the introductions are made on the first tee you will be very

tempted to let her know how good of a player you are. The urge to just blurt out that you won the "C" Flight of the 2016 Club Championship will be overwhelming, but try to resist. It's just too braggadocious. Hopefully your untucked Under Armour polo, cargo shorts and black Skechers with white footy socks are enough to send the proper signal that you're an elite player, but you can never be sure. The best medicine is to just hit a solid opening tee shot.

2. **Race by the Ladies Tee -** After you and the boys tee off, go ahead and blow by her tee box in your golf cart and head out to your ball. Women don't like the pressure of hitting in front of other people and they will appreciate your thoughtfulness. Although it's okay to start stepping off your yardage, try not to actually hit your approach shot into the green before she hits her tee ball—that could be construed as rude.

3. **Be Complimentary -** If there's one thing I've learned about women, it's that they love positive reinforcement. The more complimentary you are on the golf course, the better they feel about themselves. The trick becomes deciding which shots to compliment. A great shot for a beginning lady golfer could be very different from a great shot

for an accomplished one. I play it safe by saying, "great shot!" every time she makes contact with the ball and "good swing" on every whiff. If we're being honest, saying, "great shot" on a whiff can come off as a little patronizing.

4. **Give Lots of Putts** - Let's face it, women are not great putters. I don't know if it's an evolutionary thing or a byproduct of growing up in an environment where most of their formative years were spent shopping for jeans at the mall. Either way, females don't seem to have the same level of hand-eye coordination and "touch" that we men do. We need to be extra vigilant on how we conduct ourselves as we get near the putting surface. For instance, if she hits a great chip up to eight feet, setting up her first par putt of the round, go ahead and give it to her. The last thing you want to do is expose her to an embarrassing three-putt. On the flip side, anything over 30 feet you need to go ahead and let her putt, because giving her those might come off as condescending. It's a delicate balance. Remember, her main goal is to stay out of your way, but we men need to also remember that she paid a green fee as well.

5. **Be a Mentor** - All too often women are hesitant to ask men for help on the golf course. After all,

she just witnessed you fire a 48 on the front nine, so she has you up on a pedestal, and asking you for swing tips can be somewhat intimidating. My advice is to beat them to the punch by breaking down what they did wrong after each and every swing. She wants to get better, and you showing an interest in her swing will be a boon for her self esteem. Just throw the classics at her like "keep your head down" and "follow through." If she continues to hit poor shots, it's okay to roll your eyes or audibly sigh, but don't show your frustration outwardly.

6. **Watch the Boorish Behavior -** When a female is in the group, there are certain things you can't do or say that you normally would. Like taking a leak off the side of the tee box, or ripping a gigantic wet fart in your buddy's backswing or showing everyone the video of you pounding those two Samoan girls you met last night on Craigslist. It's simply not appropriate.

This goes for your language as well. Be careful talking to your golf ball in mid-flight. If you're someone who normally shouts expletives at your golf ball as it sails high into the trees or mockingly proclaims your homosexuality while leaving putt after putt short, that all probably needs to be dialed back a bit. Although not all women are prudes or delicate flowers, many are, so you need to be on your best behavior.

7. **Look for Cues** - I always operate under the assumption that if a woman chooses to go to a golf course alone, she is likely looking for a love connection...that's just common sense. Knowing this, always be on the lookout for little comments she makes or questions she asks that could be code for something far beyond the game of golf. For instance, if she makes any outwardly flirtatious statements during the round such as "good shot" or "nice one," or asks any provocative questions like "will you hand me the rake" or "can you laser this yardage for me," then she almost surely is totally in to you.

Caddie Breakups

My longtime caddie Ernesto left me by leaving a note in my locker that simply read, "You no make no cuts. Adios."

The Evolution of the Golf Swing

Over the years everything about the game of golf has evolved, including the swing. I follow these changes closely. Not only is it my job as an elite instructor to be in the know, it also creates new opportunities to sell my students on a complete swing teardown and rebuild. Whenever you see a cover story in a major golf magazine about a new swing phenomenon like the "Stack and Tilt" or the "X-Factor," within days teaching pros everywhere are buying timeshares, paying years of back child support and making down payments on pre-owned Sea-Doos. After these magazines hit your mailboxes, countless desperate golfers rush into the pro-shop eager to learn the secret behind a brand new, game-changing swing. Cha-ching!

As an instructor, I have to ask myself two questions before I introduce a radically different swing to a potential student. One, are they financially able to pay for a series of never-ending lessons that result in very little improvement for a minimum of six months? Two, as a teacher, do I understand the new swing concepts enough to bullshit my way through an hour-long lesson? If the answer to both of these questions is "yes," I sign that student up and get started ASAP!

The Rule That's Killing Golf (and Why You Should Break It)

LET'S BE HONEST, the USGA has a lot of ridiculous rules. From making competitors hole out every putt, to requiring players to be "super" exact when they add up their scores. It's basically like North Korea. The rule that bugs me the most is the one that limits the number of clubs a player can carry in their bag, better known as the "14 Club Rule."

Speaking as a guy who owns the shop at a semi-private country club, it's already hard enough for me to compete with other retailers. I gotta go head-to-head with golf specialty stores that offer name-brand clubs, big box retailers like Costco with better prices and more knowledgeable sales people, and online retailers where customers can avoid the high pressure sales tactics which I rely on. With only 14 available slots in the bag, there's just not a lot of opportunity for me to strong arm one of my members into a fifth wedge or an off-brand driver. But if the "suits" at the USGA pulled their heads out of their asses and got rid of this ridiculous rule, think of how many more clubs we could ALL sell.

All golfers need to be prepared for any shot and club pros need to make our nut, so let's eliminate the 14-club rule. Every golfer would benefit from having two drivers, one for distance and one for accuracy. All of us need a 3-wood, 5-wood and either a 7- or 9-wood and at least two hybrids. Driving irons are glorified regular irons that cost upwards of $200, so I'd love to sell one to every member at my club. The rest of their set should include 1-iron through pitching wedge plus a gap, sand and lob wedge. The 14-club rule has also been holding back sales of chippers and Alien wedges and these clubs are absolute stroke savers (not to mention 76-degree wedges for those full swing shots from that tricky ten to 15-yard range). On the greens give me a "feel" putter for long distances and a long putter or arm-lock for the short ones. The icing on the cake, a left handed club for trouble shots and an old, nicked-up club if you play a course that has rocky lies. That's at least 21 clubs for most golfers. If every player in America could add at least seven clubs to their set, think of the shot in the arm that would be for the golf industry! Sales, repair and re-gripping would all see massive increases. This is an absolute no-brainer, so of course, I don't have any faith that the powers that be will do the "right thing" anytime soon.

A Keen Eye for (Lack-of) Talent

IDENTIFYING STUDENTS who lack talent is easy, but only the best instructors can convince them to give up the game.

Assigning Proper Blame

ANY EVENT WHERE YOU have a partner can be a fun respite from the grind and solitude of individual medal play. Whether it's your local Member-Guest tournament or a critical four-ball match at the Ryder Cup, having a partner is always a breath of fresh air. You're part of a team. A brotherhood. You are comrades in arms.

This format is great for having your rare miscue covered up by your partner's easy par. And when your partner misfires, you are there to pay him back. You and your "pardsy" are ham and egg-ing it all around the golf course. Your somewhat risky decision to wear matching outfits never looked so good! Until it didn't. Oh, how quickly it can turn. Unbridled optimism, high-fives and chest bumps quickly turn to passive aggressive jabs and eye rolls when the chips start chunking and the putts stop dropping. Your partner's third tee ball out of bounds on the last four holes forces you to put on a body language display that screams, "Why did I invite this hack?!?!" This is roughly the point in the proceedings when it dawns on you that this disastrous round will be posted as a team score for all to see. Even though you feel like you played well, nobody will know it. You don't deserve to go down with the ship! You need to let everyone know that you pulled your weight. You need to tell everyone what the scorecard won't! But how?

Once you've turned in your card and begin milling around with the other competitors, it's time to make sure the blame gets properly assigned. But be careful, it's a delicate balance. You want to make sure everyone knows your partner was entirely responsible for your team's poor finish, but you don't want to be completely obvious about it. When someone asks you the obligatory, "How did it go out there today," here are some 'stock' responses that I recommend you answer with that seem innocuous enough, but will do the job of putting your partner securely under the bus.

1. "I played great. Unfortunately, my pardsy struggled…BIG TIME."

2. "I hit 16 greens but got zero help."

3. "You ever see a guy three-putt from eight feet twice? I have."

4. "It was a 226-yard, par-3, and all he had to do was hit the green."

5. "When am I gonna learn to stop inviting clients as partners?"

6. "We shot 82 as a team, and I shot 84 on my own ball...if that tells you anything."

7. "It's hard to be aggressive when your partner is in his pocket all day."

8. "Let's just say my back hurts."

Each one of these pre-prepared lines subtly lets your listener know that you played to your full potential and it was your partner who was a complete no-show. Feel free to either memorize these lines or write them down and keep them on hand.

Trying to "Make It"

TO ME, THERE'S NOTHING in the game of golf more amusing than a young man who actually believes he's good enough to play on the PGA Tour. The pure delusion of it is a sight to behold. Every few years here at the club we get a member's son who returns from a mediocre playing career in college and starts hitting up potential investors so he can go "chase the dream." These are the kids who shoot effortless 66s on their home course with a cooler full of Michelob Ultras in the cart and the bluetooth speaker going, but then shoot 81-76 in the State Am when it actually matters. Imagine how naive you have to be to fire a 79 in local U.S. Open qualifying and then immediately head down to Florida and attempt to Monday at the Honda Classic using someone else's money. Unless it's a Korean female, I tell every young person who comes to see me about playing golf for a living the same thing...start studying for your insurance license exam.

Are You Good Enough to Get Angry?

HAVE I EVER LOST my temper on the course? Uh... yes. I'll never forget the 1991 Mexicali Masters when I three-putted from four feet to miss the cut by one and helicoptered my Maxfli "Black Max" putter into a hospitality tent where it struck a churro vendor in the temple. Anger is part of the game.

When you play at an elite level ("C" flight or higher), you have high expectations, and when you fail to meet those expectations, that anger is going to come out one way or another. In my opinion, damaging your equipment or exploding on your playing partners is a very healthy way to exorcise your demons.

It's been said that most golfers are "not good enough to get mad," but I totally disagree. You're at the golf course to escape the bullshit of your day-to-day life, but that isn't a one-way street. If you have a disappointing round, you can bring that anger home with you. Destroying a tee marker, repeatedly stabbing the green with a broken shaft or shouting hate filled expletives for a minute straight without catching your breath are all healthy, normal ways to channel the frustrations of playing poorly. It also keeps the lingering effects of a bad round from settling into your psyche.

Don't take my word for it. The next time you lose a bet thanks to a three-putt on the 18th hole, you can bite your lip and shake your opponent's hand or you can beat the plexiglass windshield of your cart into oblivion. You tell me which one leaves you feeling more satisfied.

My Lesson with El Chapo

Being a "pretty big deal" in Mexico during the '90s meant crossing paths with some pretty important people. One such person was noted philanthropist and mass murderer Joaquin "El Chapo" Guzman. I met El Chapo during a Monday qualifier at the 1995 Culiacán Skins Game. When I pulled up to the drivable par-4, 12th hole, it was stacked up with three groups on the tee. This short stocky guy (who turned out to be El Chapo) notices my Cougar Staff Bag and asks me if I'm a pro. I tell him who I am and he immediately starts hitting me up for swing tips. After showing me his move I notice he's coming way over the top. I told him the 24-carat gold, 9mm Glock under his right armpit is causing his right elbow to fly out, producing a big left to right ball fight and a loss of distance.

I had him move the holster to his left side and he immediately starts hitting these penetrating baby draws. Total piss missiles. Chapo can move it out there for a smaller guy, but I later heard his short game is atrocious. Long story short, he took down my name and told me as long as I'm in Mexico I would receive safe passage. I never had one problem after that.

Merchandising

AS A CLUB PRO I'm more than just an elite player, I'm also required to be a great businessman. I own the shop here at my club and take merchandising very seriously. Unlike many of my fellow club pros, I don't believe in fancy corporate buzzwords like "paying taxes" or "profit." I believe in members looking their best, so they can play their best. It hasn't always gone smoothly.

Back in 2012, I decided to go "all in" and transform our retail space into a Tabasco/Chiliwear concept shop. Turns out no one was willing to pay $119.99 for a full coverage graphic polo of an American flag mixed with a Hawaiian sunset being drenched in hot sauce.

I don't carry many of the "name" brands because I consider myself more of a boutique shop and I have massive credit issues. PING, Taylormade and Callaway won't call on me because they say I "don't pay them." Agree to disagree. It's all corporate doublespeak and the good ol' boy network. The golf merchandise world is very political.

The Dreaded Fried Egg— Time to Cook Up an Excuse

WE'VE ALL BEEN THERE, your normally reliable Orlimar 7-wood finally lets you down by producing a weak, wipey fade that finds the green-side bunker. Upon arriving at your ball, you're shocked to find it in a buried lie, or what we in "the biz" like to call a fried egg. While other so-called teaching pros might offer you techniques for how to execute this shot, I prefer to take the more realistic approach by informing you that you don't have the talent to get this shot up and down —period. So let's just focus on what you can control: playing the victim. Follow these three steps for playing fried-egg lies and in no time you'll have a fool-proof excuse for hitting lousy bunker shots.

1. **Spread the Word -** Once you've identified your lie you have only one job, and that's to make sure every one of your playing partners is fully aware of your misfortune. This is paramount. They need to know that what happens next will absolutely not be your fault. How to do this? You could start shouting expletives, but this is a gentleman's game. Instead, stand in the bunker with your hands on your hips, motionless over the ball as you stare at the lie in dismay. This can go on for anywhere from five to 90 seconds, but it's critical that you hold the position until someone in your group acknowledges there's an issue. Mercifully, one of your playing partners will eventually say something along the lines of, "Dude, are you buried?"

2. **Point the Finger -** Once everyone is aware of your bad break, you're playing with house money. It's time to assign blame. As you dig your feet into the sand, take aim at the grounds crew by blurting something like, "The last trap I was in was pure hardpan, now this?!" or "We blow money on remodeling the ladies locker room, all the while we're rocking the worst bunkers in the city?!" or, "The greenskeeper here is a laughingstock!"

3. **Fake the Heads-Up -** Even though you've now artfully apprised the group of your lie predica-

ment, the charade needs one last flourish. It's what I like to call "The Warning." A second before you start your takeaway, say something pithy to make 100-percent certain your foursome knows this will not be an easy shot. Something like, "OK, guys, put your heads on a swivel," or "Watch your dental work, bros!" Or my favorite: the lamentably underused, "Heads-up! This could go anywhere!" Once you pull the trigger and, predictably, leave your rock on the beach, finish off the show by reaching for the rake and muttering something like, "That's all I could do." In three simple steps you'll have achieved your goal of lowering expectations for your short-game to something close to zero.

A Lesson in Lessons

THERE ARE DAYS when I have lessons booked with students who I know have zero chance of improving, but for some reason we go through with the charade anyway.

How I Make Money

WHETHER YOU AGREE or disagree that club professionals are overpaid is a subject for another book. I make $42,000 a year and I'll be the first to admit that I'm extremely blessed. Not a day goes by that I don't thank my lucky stars for how high I've climbed in the industry. I'd say in golf's pecking order, being the head pro at a semi-private golf club ranks somewhere between Brandel Chamblee's personal assistant and Lexi Thompson's boy toy. It's a pretty sweet spot to be. I meet a lot of young kids who want to get where I'm at, and the first thing they ask about is money. They've all seen my ride, heard stories about my timeshare in Branson, and know that I play Lynx "Black Cat" irons. They know I'm not hurting. What a lot of people don't realize is that my already bloated salary makes up just a portion of my income. Here are a few ways that club pros like myself supplement our income.

Lost and Found - This is my honey hole. The lost and found is a literal goldmine for club professionals. Thanks to expensive range finders, bluetooth speakers and even collectible head-covers, the pickings are getting more lucrative by the day.

Upgraded Golf Shafts - These are the cryptocurrency of the golf world. My members have ZERO idea what they're getting and they are literally willing to pay through the nose. Eventually this house of cards is gonna collapse, but I'm going to keep riding it until it does. Hell, I've even got some members asking me about custom putter shafts - Hedonism Resort here I come!

Staff Clubs - I get most of my equipment for cost plus ten percent. It's a very sweet deal. Let's just say this contributes to my very active eBay account.

Lessons and Clinics - Here's where the real money comes in! I especially love junior clinics. I spend five minutes showing the kids how to grip the club and then leave my assistants to babysit them while I get ready to work the line of moms in minivans picking them up. I am blessed.

Spiffs - Most of you don't know this but golf manufacturers will often pay us cash bonuses for selling their clubs. These are called spiffs. It incentivizes pros like myself to throw all fitting data out the window and strong arm members into buying a club that earns me a small cash bonus. If I can make an extra $10 selling you a driver even though it feels (and performs) like a 2x4, that's a tradeoff I'm willing to live with.

The Dreaded Slice

If you're reading this, chances are you're a guy who struggles with a persistent and uncontrollable slice. There are many reasons for this, but first and foremost is the fact that you don't possess the God-given athletic ability necessary to swing the golf club in a manner that produces a solid ball flight.

The mistake that so many amateurs make is actually believing that they can somehow fix it. They think if they watch enough YouTube videos, buy enough training aids or hit enough range balls, they can somehow "will" themselves into hitting penetrating draws. I hate to be the guy to break it to you, but it ain't happening.

I know it sounds overly simplistic, but you just need to aim left. Yes, it's true that aiming left only helps to promote a bigger slice but I have an easy workaround for that: aim farther left.

Provisionals

DURING MY TENURE on the Mexican Mini-Tour, nobody hit more provisionals than I did. Was that because I hit a lot of wayward shots? Yes. But a little-known secret is that many of the provisionals I hit on tour were for quite another reason. And that reason was the need for In-Round Practice (IRP).

As a competitor, you have to understand that there will be times during your round when you begin to feel your swing start to get away from you. This is commonly referred to as, "the wheels coming off." Unfortunately, when this happens you can't just call a 'timeout' and head over to the driving range for a quick fix. You have to find your swing another way, and that's by hitting a slew of provisionals.

Let's say you hook a drive into the left rough. Even though you know it's clearly in-bounds, you don't want to leave the tee box with the bad taste of that swing lingering in your mouth. You need to hit another tee ball ASAP to get your swing back on track. So announce to your playing competitors that your first ball could be O.B. (or lost) and you are electing to hit a provisional. The beauty of this is that nobody can stop you. If you claim your ball could be out of play they have to take your word for it (LOL).

When my swing really needs some work and I'm certain my first ball is in play I may go ahead and aim out of bounds and intentionally pump seven or eight balls O.B. so I can continue to hit until I feel like my swing is grooved again.

Music on the Course

As A TOP CLUB professional, one of my responsibilities is acting like I care about "Growing the Game," so from time to time I do a little something to help. That means doing my part to make what has traditionally been known as a stuffy sport for rich a-holes to be more attractive to younger generations. One thing I've learned over the years is that so called "Millennials" and the even younger "Gen Z" crowd are all about loosening up the "vibe" on the golf course.

In addition to untucked t-shirts, non-stop vaping, and an immeasurable sense of entitlement, these kids gotta have music on the course, and I have to tell you, I'm not sold. We've all been there, you're on the first tee paired up with some "fun guy" who's fiddling with a Bluetooth speaker and you know the question is coming: "Mind if I play some music?"

Here's where you lose me, pardsy; that's not the right question to ask. All music isn't created equal. Asking if I want to hear some tunes without telling me what you plan to play is like a blind date asking if I want to "watch a little porn," and the next thing I know I'm seeing a bunch of overweight Germans shitting in each other's mouths.

Sure, I'll consider some music, but what are you playing? If it's contemporary country or show tunes...I'll pass. If it's a steady diet of Def Leppard, Guns N' Roses or maybe some yacht rock, then get that speaker paired up!

My Private Cache of Swing Thoughts

During a moment of boredom on the driving range at the 1993 Todos Santos Open, my caddie Ernesto playfully tossed an iron cover at my head as I was hitting a shot. Caught by surprise, I instinctively jerked my head backwards and contorted my body in an effort to avoid the incoming foreign object. Much to my amazement, that swing resulted in a mammoth drive that went far down the range. Intrigued, I asked him to do it again. Once again Ernesto threw an object at my head during my swing and, again, the drive went far and true. This process was repeated throughout an entire monster bucket of balls. Convinced that I had "found" something, I coined this swing thought, "dodgeball" and went to the first tee full of confidence and ready to put it in play. Sadly, when Ernesto tossed a divot repair tool at my face during my opening tee shot, I hit a massive pull hook out-of-bounds. I tell you this story as a cautionary tale. Although swing thoughts are the DNA of every elite golfer's game, and serve as the glue that holds a golf swing together, their effectiveness can sometimes be fleeting. As quickly as they appear, they can be gone.

However, like an old putter that you pull out of the garage that still has a few putts left in it, I save all my old swing thoughts in case they work again in the future. As you're reading this right now consider yourself very fortunate. It's extremely rare that a player of my caliber opens up their private vault of swing thoughts, especially for free. Here are just a few of the swing thoughts I have used in competition throughout my career on the Mexican Mini-Tour:

- Thumbs up 7-UP.
- Hold on tight.
- Let it go.
- The club is a snake.
- Left elbow points towards mama's house.
- My wrist is a bowl of soup.
- You're giving a high-five.
- Scratch that itch.
- Turn around a stick up your ass.
- Step on the Coke can.
- To hit a draw, make your elbows see-saw.
- Check the watch. Hold it. Now it's go time.
- You're inside a jar of honey.
- Don't go right, don't go right, don't go right... FUCK!
- Face down, ass up.
- Just like Sunday School.
- Ice, ice, baby.
- Bust a nut in the teacup.
- Lietzke '81.
- Juice boy!
- Ring that dinner bell.
- Turn to dance with Susie.
- Let your kneecaps talk back.
- Right heel, you've been a bad boy.
- Left pants pocket full of Cracker Jacks.
- Belt buckle don't lie. Then let it fly.

- Turn. Wait, what? Hammer time.
- You're shucking an oyster.
- Right foot on hot coals.
- Open the tuna can.
- Right back pocket is lava.
- Give your wedge a speech impediment.
- Wax on, but don't wax off.
- Jerry Sandusky.
- Was that a pop? Then GO!

The Retired Member Guy

EVERY CLUB HAS one. The guy that walks into the shop on a random Tuesday morning wearing his gleaming white New Balance sneakers, Nautica t-shirt, and carpenter jean shorts. All of us in the shop cringe when he enters because we know he's not here to quickly check in and head to the first tee. We know he's not here to play golf at all. He's here for something much worse...he's here to "shoot the shit."

Oh, he tries to not make it obvious. He starts by moseying over to the club bulletin board to check the Glo-Ball League stats, then he fills up a styrofoam cup of coffee and begins to peruse a few apparel items on the 70 percent off rack and mutter how overpriced everything still is, but this is all theater.

The real reason for his visit emerges as he saunters up to the counter and asks my assistant if he "saw the game last night." When he says, "no" and pretends to work on the tee sheet, some people might get the signal. The "retired member guy" is undaunted. He takes another sip of free coffee as he casually grabs a Snake Eyes putter off the rack and takes a few practice strokes with it. Then he meanders into my office, where my inability to close the door completely when I arrived that morning is a mistake I am about to pay dearly for.

Never mind that my back is to him and I'm working on my computer. He comes right in and takes a chair. Do I turn around? No. Do I acknowledge him? No. Does it phase him? No. Listen, I know that he's retired. I get that his wife is more tired of his bullshit than even I am. I know that he's bored. I get it, but that doesn't give him license to come in to my office during my workday and spend 40-minutes bitching to me about how high gas prices are, or how his brother-in-law just got a set of PXGs, or how he knows a guy who knows a guy who went on a trip to Whistling Straits.

NOBODY CARES about ANY of this. Please make it stop.

Taking an Inventory of Your Game

At the end of every golf season I like to take stock of my game by analyzing the scores I posted versus the scores I didn't post. The results can be eye opening.

Growing the Game

I get it—we need to "Grow the Game." You wouldn't believe how many blue-hairs I see drop dead on the golf course year after year. I know we need new, young golfers to replace the dead ones, but I'm not about to beg people to play this game and I'm certainly not going to resort to gimmicks.

Whether it's Golden Tee, miniature golf, a night out at Top Golf or seeing Tiger's "dick pics" online, everyone in America has had at least a brush with the game. If that's enough to get them interested in picking up golf as a new hobby...great! Send them on down to the course and I'll coach 'em up. When we start talking about using giant cups, six hole rounds, and discounted green fees for juniors in order to get them hooked...count me out.

The reality is, I don't think we're that desperate.

The tee sheet at my club is jam packed every day! I see absolutely no need to make the game more "accessible" to the uninitiated. That's what playground basketball courts are for! You want access? Go play disk golf with all the other stoners. It's totally free and there's no dress code. The last thing this great game needs is a bunch of entitled, woke, Gen Z pussies taking over and instituting things like allowing dogs on the course, letting juniors tee-off before two p.m. and promoting fucking Foot Golf (don't even get me started). So, yeah, when my tee sheet is empty and the 150th ranked player on the PGA money list isn't making $3 million a year, maybe we can start talking about growing the game. For now, I think we're good.

The Right Shaft May Be the Wrong Shaft

EVEN THOUGH YOU can't hit it, there's nothing more rewarding than telling people you have an X-stiff shaft in your driver.

Managment 101

A GOOD CLUB PRO supports his staff. He doesn't turn them in for petty theft or for having sex with members.

Pick It Up or Putt It?

Pick it up if:
- You feel like it's in the universally accepted "good" range.
- Your first putt is flying past the hole and may travel out of the universally accepted "gimme" range.
- It's a borderline gimme but you feel like you might miss it.
- Your opponent is not paying attention.
- You feel like you'd definitely make it anyway and/or you deserve to make it.

Putt it if:
- It's so short you have zero chance of missing it.
- It's so long that picking it up and acting like it's good would look ridiculous.
- The hole has already been won or lost.

Private Country Club Etiquette

CONGRATULATIONS! You finally got an invite to that exclusive country club you've been waiting for. It pays to have a brother-in-law with connections. After years of changing shoes in the parking lot and showing your receipt to the starter at the local muni, you've hit the big time. But before you do, there are some things you need to know that will help you fit in. There's nothing worse than looking like the "rookie" at a fancy club. You're going to need to act like you've swum in these waters before. Speaking as a club professional at a semi-private facility, I deal with my share of high rollers on a daily basis. So follow my tips below and you'll be looking like a fifth-generation blue blood in no time.

1. **Exude confidence -** As the bag boy is opening the hatch on your 1999 Toyota Corolla, seamlessly hand him a dollar bill and ask him what the greens are stimped at today. He'll immediately know this aint your first rodeo.

2. **Blend in** - Even though you're not a member, it's important to let people know that you're no schmuck. As you walk through the clubhouse to the men's locker room, put your phone to your ear and talk loudly in "business speak," so everyone from the cooks in the grill room to the housewives in the fitness center can hear you. Say something like, "I can get those made in China, but we'll never get them through customs by December," or "If the NASDAQ shows any more weakness, we'll have to tweak our derivatives."

3. **Set boundaries** - When you meet your caddie on the range, be cordial, but make sure he knows he's a lower status than you. The friendlier you get with him now, the tougher it will be to berate him for his green-reading skills later. Also, don't be afraid to demand that he give you distances down to the half-yard. Tell him you didn't get down to a 12-handicap by hitting shots from "about" 150.

4. **Don't be afraid to name drop** - You need to impress the member who invited you by letting him know that you're somewhat connected to his world. Say something like, "This place is nice but my boss played Kemper Lakes in Chicago a few years ago and he said it was mint," or, "I see you guys allow women here...thanks Obama."

5. **Stop and smell the roses** - You're not going to get many opportunities to play a private club, so slow down and take it all in. Be methodical. Make sure to read all of your putts from four different angles—twice. Also, take full advantage of the yardage book. Even though you've never used one before and have no idea how to read it, study it prior to every shot, even making notes in it when necessary.

Endorsements

BEING AN ELITE PLAYER means companies are dying to have you represent their products. Truth be told, back in the mid-90s most of my income came from endorsements. I had a deal with Nitro Golf Balls, an on-again, off-again, highly dysfunctional relationship with Cougar, a ball retriever company called "IGotchaGolf" and of course Yonex.

The deal with Yonex was a nice collaboration, but it ended badly. Long story short, I convinced them to make a line of "players" woods that intentionally didn't have a sweet spot. The idea behind it was that the more difficult it was to hit, the more intriguing it would be for the better player (similar to the concept behind forged irons). I even came up with the marketing slogan, "You think you're a ball striker? Let's see if you can hit this."

Needless to say it didn't work out. Even though Yonex and I parted ways and they sued me in Federal Court for breaching my fiduciary duty, I continued to play that driver for the next six years.

Is Custom Fitting Right for You?

THE RISE OF CUSTOM fittings is one of the best things to happen to the golf biz in the last twenty years, but not for the reason you might think. Subjecting the Average Joe to a three-hour custom fitting session only accomplishes two things: his back is going to be wrecked for a week and I've generated $2,000 in up-charges, fees and unnecessary options. Unfortunately for him, neither of those things is going to help him shoot lower scores, but I just covered the yearly nut on my timeshare.

The average player I see is struggling with major issues like chunked shots, the chip yips, shanks, and monster slices that don't stay on the course. There's not a custom shaft in the world that can fix those issues. The dirty little secret is I'm just handing you random shafts until you miraculously catch one solid.

Here's another nugget for you: most of the time when I'm fitting a shaft to a player I just pick the one with a color that matches his favorite team and act like it's a coincidence. He's happy that his new driver looks flashy and I don't have to pretend to know what "smash factor" is. The same is true for adjustable clubs. Look in the mirror, do you really think you're good enough to notice the difference between the B7 and the A4 setting on your driver? In the end we're only twisting the grip anyway.

Money Talks

I HAVE ZERO RESPECT for a junior player who refuses to gamble on the golf course.

A Game of Honor

One of the truly unique aspects about the game of golf is that we are encouraged, or some might even say obligated, to call penalties on ourselves. How crazy is that—leaving it up to the players to police themselves? Do you think an NFL lineman would ever call a holding penalty on himself? Hell no!

It's just one of those quirky things that makes our game so great. I played nearly a thousand competitive rounds over the course of my 14-year tour career and during that time I found myself in countless situations where I either knowingly or unknowingly broke the rules. It happens. The trick is deciding if and when to call a penalty.

For example, if I was early in a round that hadn't quite gone off the rails yet and my ball moved after I carelessly pulled a small twig out from under it, there's no way I would call that. Doing so would potentially ruin the round and might jeopardize any chance I had of making the cut. However, if it's late in a round and I've already logged a bunch of doubles and triples and I inadvertently touched the sand in a bunker, I'll definitely call that penalty on myself. Why? Because the round is meaningless at that point and it's a perfect opportunity for me to show my opponents that I have the character to call a penalty even though I'm the only one to see the infraction. It's that type of honor that truly separates golf from all the other sports.

My Eight-Hole Par Streak

LIKE PLAYING BLACKJACK, betting on college football or chasing ass in Mexico City, golf is a game of hot streaks. One moment you're plodding along trading pars for bogeys and the next thing you know, BAM! You catch a heater. Since I played so long on tour, I had more than my share of nice runs, but NOTHING could have prepared me for what I experienced during the second round of the 1998 Yucatan Masters.

The front nine was nothing out of the ordinary. I went out in 44 after making a really bad double on hole nine that included a penalty for playing a range ball. I get to the tenth tee and I'm absolutely fuming. I turn to my caddie, Ernesto, and tell him to get the scuba gear out because I'm taking it deep on the back side. After tough-luck bogeys on ten, 11 and 13, I par the last five including a nifty bump-and-run chip in on 18 to shoot 83 and miss the cut by 12. I then par the opening three holes the next Thursday at the Matamoros Four-Ball to run the par streak to eight. I've done a lot of special things on the golf course, but that streak ranks right up there.

Lesson Terminology

WHEN YOU TAKE YOUR CAR into the shop to get it serviced and hear the mechanic use words like "engine manifold," "fuel injectors," and "chassis," it gives you a sense of confidence that he is an expert in his field and that you and your car are in very good hands. It's the same thing with a golf lesson. When I am with a student, I have an array of terms that I use on a loop. Such as "single plane," "supination," "Moment of Inertia" (MOI), "spine angle," and "lag." Like you, I have little to no idea what these terms mean or how to practically apply them. Since you just pre-paid $600 for a season-long lesson package, I feel obliged to use them liberally throughout the process.

Getting "Comfortable" with Training Aids

For me, training aids like pool noodles and hula hoops are what a hammer and nails are to a carpenter.

It wasn't always like that. I learned golf the traditional way—by hitting countless balls with old, heavy, beat-up clubs and a healthy dose of verbal abuse from my instructor. In my days on tour I rolled my eyes at the "soft" golfers who were looking for shortcuts by incorporating training aids into their practice. I treated practice as painful, mindless, drudgery which resulted in little improvement and plentiful blisters. I was (and maybe still am) old school. But my opinion on training aids changed in the blink of an eye in 1992.

After a missed cut in Mexico City, I got roped into a big money game at a local course. Long story short, it was a set-up by a couple of cartel-affiliated sandbaggers, and when I didn't have the money to pay my debt, they made me a deal: carry a few bags of dope for them to the next tour stop in Acapulco and I'd get to keep my thumbs. They'd even pay to fly me. Win, win! I was already dabbling in a tiny bit of "mule work" on the side that season (and a few others), which was a good little chunk of passive income that helped me stay afloat.

I'm not ashamed to admit I shoved the package up my ass. I'm not alone. There are plenty of major champions and tour poster boys that I can guarantee have boarded a jet with a few extra passengers hidden in the trunk. (I can tell by the distant look in their eyes. Anyway, the things we do to make it on tour. Ha!)

The problem came when my plane was stuck on the tarmac for two hours. When I landed, I didn't have time to crap 'em out and raced straight to the tee for the first round of the tournament. That's when something crazy happened. I was straining so hard to keep the balloons from shooting out of my ass that my core was fully engaged. Talk about activating your glutes. Five hours and 73 strokes later, I had played my best round of golf that season. To this day I've never hit the ball as good as I did during that round.

Back in the hotel, after the best crap of my life, I was lying in bed. If a few simple balloons of horse shoved up my keister could make that big of a difference in my play, what other solutions were out there? The rest is history. So if you come see me in the Learning Center and I pull out a coat hanger, a basketball or even a stuffed balloon, relax and prepare to let the learning in!

A Day in the Life

A LOT OF PEOPLE THINK club pros lead a "baller" lifestyle because they have that moniker of "professional" attached to their title. That may be somewhat true, but to be totally honest, my day-to-day life can be fairly mundane. Let's take yesterday for example. I opened the doors at 6 a.m., spent 7 to 8:45 a.m. taking a dump in the ladies locker room, conducted a super-seniors flop shot clinic from 10 a.m. to noon, took a nap in the bag room, assembled a Top-Flite Magna display until 2 p.m., met with the Aureus apparel rep until 4 p.m., then spent the remainder of the afternoon dotting scorecards for that evening's Three-Club Mixed Couples Twilight Shamble. Finally, I hand-picked the range until dark, had eight Zimas and four lap dances at Bottoms Up, got back to my condo at 12:30 a.m., jerked it, and then called it a day.

Match Play Mindset

In match play, always expect your opponent to hit a great shot. And when they do, pack it in baby, because that hole is probably lost.

Getting the Most out of Playing by Yourself

I love playing alone. There aren't many sports you can play by yourself and, after a day of dealing with my idiot members, a little solo time on the course is much appreciated. When I play as a single I like to let my mind wander, pondering things like, if I added a spoiler to my Miata how much more ass could I pull in? Or, if just another 20-25 putts dropped would I have won the 1992 Yucatan Masters? Or, how will our beverage cart girl Anastasia Adams' massive rack hold up in ten years? You know, the big questions in life. While unplugging is great, playing solo is also a phenomenal time to put in some work on your game.

With no one there to keep you honest it's pretty easy to lose focus, so I like to create some imaginary stakes to keep my head in the game. Like pretending I'm playing a simulated tournament in my head. Just don't go overboard with the fantasy scenarios—it's too much pressure and a little ridiculous. We've all played a hole and said to ourselves, "All he needs is a par here to win The Masters." Instead, try to grind out a bogey to "make the cut on the number at the Barbasol Championship." Or imagine you need three putts from 20 feet to avoid a last-place finish in a Korn Ferry event. Have fun, make it challenging, but keep things somewhat realistic.

If it's the end of the day and you're the only one out there, grab 10 or 15 balls off the driving range and head out to work on a few different shots. Using range balls is critical because it's obviously no big deal if you lose them. The last thing you want to do is waste valuable daylight looking for your own gamers in the rough.

Also, make sure to put in some work in the bunkers, because there's no need to rake them at this time of night. In fact, you really don't have to do much of anything knowing that the maintenance crew is coming back in about eight short hours. Let THEM replace the beaver-pelt divots you left all over the back nine, let THEM fix the ball marks from the

12 towering wedges you shelled the 16th green with. That's what they're paid for!

The bottom line is, these are times for experimentation. Change things up. Do you draw the ball? Try to hit a fade. Have you ever tried to Stack and Tilt? Go for it! Always thought about putting cross-handed? Give it a try. Best case scenario, you make a huge breakthrough. Worst case, you screw up your game for a year and have to come see me to undo the damage. Most important of all, post your score and make it count. There's not a soul around to verify whether you shot 72 or 102. If you're a vanity handicap guy, great round! If you're like me and like to keep the index super high for wagering purposes, it was another tough day.

Staying Cool When Going Low

I'M ALWAYS AMAZED at how many of my students are simply afraid to go low. If you manage to get it to four or five under (net) par, EMBRACE IT!

How to Carry Yourself on the Golf Course

IT'S A FACT, YOU gotta look good to play good. I'm a firm believer that your swagger and style has a huge impact on your score. I'm no stranger to turning heads on the golf course because I carry myself like the club professional that I am. To get here took years of observation and practicing all the little things that elite players do to set themselves apart from amateurs like yourself. Even though your game isn't nearly as good as mine, if you try to integrate a few of my habits, mannerisms and style pointers into your repertoire, good things can start to happen for you too.

Style
- White belts only. You might say that's a look from the 70s, but trust me, it's coming back.
- I love my FJ sandals - they're my daily drivers, but if I'm out there to step on some necks, I'm playing in Dexter saddles—a timeless look that means business.
- Try to integrate some kind of flair. I like those copper bracelets that make your wrist turn green.

It proves that they work. Otherwise try to wear some KT tape or some type of forearm brace. Also, wrap the bottom of your right index finger with white tape like Tiger does. If you want to really go next level, add a coral choker necklace.
- Finish it off with some nice shades. While the younger crowd prefers Oakleys, I'm an unapologetic Blue Blocker guy.

Gear

- Slap some lead tape on something, anything. How will it affect your club? Who cares, but it looks cool as shit and lets your opponent know you've calibrated your sticks to within an inch of their life.
- Get yourself some Tour Velvet grips. They wear out fast, are way too smooth and are worthless in the rain, but they're in almost every bag on Tour (The Champions Tour).
- Carry at least one unhittable club in your bag purely for intimidation. Like an old 1-iron, a persimmon 2-wood or a 68-degree wedge.
- If you clean your clubs with anything other than a stolen hotel towel you're a hack. Period.

Swagger
- Always, always, always leave your left foot dangling outside the golf cart while driving.
- Never call anyone by their actual name. It's either "pards," "guy," "pro," or some variation of their name with "y" added to the end, (Tommy, Mikey, Smitty).
- Always take a golf cart and insist on driving. If you must carry your own bag, make sure the clubs point backwards not forwards.
- Mark your ball with a poker chip, but it must be from an ACTUAL casino (and at least $5 denomination). This sends a clear message: if you're a guy who's willing to walk out of a casino without cashing a $5 chip, then there's certainly not a wager on the golf course that is going to intimidate you.

The Power of Language In Match Play

MATCH PLAY IS A frustrating format because no matter how good you play, it can be very difficult to win holes. This is especially true against better players.

If you find yourself in a match play situation where you are clearly outgunned, then it might be time to resort to some guerilla tactics that have been very effective for me over the years. Chief among those techniques is using language to cause your opponent to lose holes on technicalities.

Midway through my career as part of an unyielding quest to get better, I did some work with a board-certified audiologist and learned some incredible things about the characteristics of sound waves and how the brain reacts and processes them. For instance, did you know that the difference between phrases such as "that's good" and "bats could" is almost indistinguishable to the human ear? Same thing goes for "You're away," and "Uruguay." As a result of my training I discovered that mumbling to your opponent can cause confusion, which can be used to your advantage.

If an opponent picks up a six-inch putt after you mumble, "bats could," guess what? You just won a critical hole. If an opponent stuffs an approach shot to four feet after hearing you say, "Uruguay." Guess what? He just played out of turn and needs to replay his shot. You get the idea. "Pita cup" sure sounds like "pick-it-up" to me.

Playing great golf is certainly a valuable tool when it comes to being an accomplished match-play player, but the power of language is what truly separates the best from the rest.

Developing a Go-To Shot

I don't care if you're Tiger Woods or a D-Flight chop, every golfer needs a shot they can rely on when they're under the gun. For me, it's the laser-like accuracy of my provisional tee ball; for Tiger, it's his patented "stinger;" for Jordan Spieth, it's his aggressive mid-range putting; and for Patrick Reed, it's improving his lie in a waste area or taking an illegal drop. Find or develop a shot or skill that you can count on when you need it most.

Playing in the Zone

There's no better feeling than being completely dialed in. When I'm playing my absolute best I sometimes don't even remember taking my iron cover off and on before and after a shot.

Fighting the First-Tee Jitters

I HATE TO ADMIT IT, but for years I battled the first- tee jitters. I'm courageously sharing this with you now, so you don't feel so bad when you inevitably choke on your next, big opening tee shot. When a player of my caliber struggles with this, it just goes to show how big of an obstacle it can be.

The jitters come from a fear of embarrassment. You're worried onlookers will see you hit a shitty drive and think you're not a very good player. Guess what? You're not a very good player! If you have anything to be embarrassed about it should be that CaboWabo polo shirt you're wearing that you got at the airport on spring break nine years ago, not your golf swing. However, there are a few techniques that you can employ that might help you feel more comfortable as you set up for this nervy shot.

1. **Preparation** - Prepare yourself for the worst shot possible. That way when it happens, you're not taken by surprise. Freedom comes with acceptance.

2. **Strategize Your Reaction -** When your ball inevitably goes 60 yards dead left into the club swimming pool, onlookers will be keen to see your reaction. Will you shrink in embarrassment? Will you laugh at yourself? Will you go on a profanity-laced tirade? It's always good to have a plan because the last thing you want to do is reflexively shatter a tee marker in anger with your driver or go on a racist/homophobic rant, forcing you leave the club for 90 days to "educate yourself and listen."

3. **Protect Scarce Resources -** Lastly, don't use a new ball. This shot is hard enough. Using a perfectly Sharpied Pro V1x just ratchets up the pressure and makes you feel worse when it lasts exactly one swing. Instead use that Noodle that's been banging around in the bottom of your bag until you get your sea legs under you.

The Camera Doesn't Lie

CAMERA PHONES HAVE been a boon to the teaching profession. Look at any golf swing in slow motion. I don't care how bad the player is, it looks like there are some good things happening. There's some rotation, the club is loading, and there's that satisfying clunk at impact.

Bottom line, with video I can convince any student that they're a few inches of shoulder turn or left pants pocket rotation away from absolutely striping it. Just a couple more lessons and they're there!

As an added bonus, half the time I'm "filming" one of my students during a lesson I'm either placing a bet, on a porn site, or tweeting. Thanks, Steve Jobs!

Picking the Right Putter

THEY SAY CLOTHES make the man. I say the putter makes the golfer. Here's what your putter says about you and which putter you should be using.

Old School 8802 Putter - We get it, you could break 80 back in the day and think you're getting to scratch someday. Sorry to break it to you, but your days of shooting 72, like your hairline, are long gone and aren't coming back. Cut the shit, pry open your wallet and buy a putter that was made in this millennium and maybe you'll turn that 85 into a 79.

Mallet Putter - These putters have a larger, forgiving face for off-center hits. Perfect for the stylish pragmatist who still won't drain that clutch ten-footer on the 18th hole.

High MOI Putter - These massive putters feature adjustable weights, high MOI (which stands for Moment of Impact) and bold aiming lines. These are designed for golfers who can't make short putts. Like those who use oversized grips or are experimenting with "the claw" or some other bullshit putting stroke, high MOI putters are just stopgaps before finally resorting to using a long putter or quitting the game and taking up mountain biking.

Scotty Cameron or Small-Shop, Custom Putter - I see a lot of my club's players trotting out fancy, "boutique" putters from guys like Scott Cameron, Bettinardi something, and others. Let me let you all in on a secret: THEY'RE ALL RIDING ON THE COATTAILS OF KARSTEN SOLHEIM'S 50-YEAR-OLD DESIGN! Just get a Ping Anser from a garage sale instead, and buy a new driver with the hundreds of dollars you just saved.

Long Putter/Arm Lock Putter - I love the long putter for amateur players because you're telling the world, "I can't putt for shit." Your bold admission of weakness is your strength and, in this day and age, if your opponent makes you putt out the short ones, it's basically a violation of the Americans with Disabilities Act. Use that to your advantage.

The Difference Between Tour Pros and Club Pros

THERE ARE ALMOST 30,000 PGA professionals out there and I'm here to tell you, we've got game for days. Many of us long walked the same path as the Nicklauses, Woods, and Don Blake's of the world: a shelf full of junior golf trophies, success while bouncing around multiple junior colleges and local charity scrambles, participation in countless USGA qualifiers, and cashing checks on the mini-tours. But that's where our paths diverge. The reality is, the difference between making millions on the PGA Tour and "folding shirts" in the pro shop is razor thin.

Let me break it down for you regular folks. On a recent trip to Branson, I visited a course where the staff was buzzing about a PGA Tour stud who had just torched the place with a 71. This player (I won't say his name, but he's known for wearing more than one golf glove when he plays) was there for a bachelor party, totally blitzed and played in flip-flops, but a 71 is still seriously golfing your ball. When I played the very same track I proceeded to fire my own little 82. Not even close you say? Let's take a closer look.

I was playing the Sorenstam Tees which are about 1,650-yards shorter than the Daly Tees that he played, but according to a cart boy I spoke to, the angles in from the Sorenstams are much, much more demanding. During the round I hit three tee shots OB (including one which hit a condo hard and came within inches of bouncing back in bounds). If that wasn't a bad enough break, I also had a four-putt after burning the edge on my first attempt. Lastly, I was chipping in my timeshare the night before, and like an idiot, I left my Square Strike wedge in the living room. I was fully under-equipped, and as a direct result, I duffed two chips.

Let's do the math, a couple of bad driver swings, a bullshit lip-out, and a gear issue, (which BTW happens to the tour guys ALL THE TIME, but they have a truck full of replacement clubs on site) cost me 11 strokes. I also dunked two balls into the water and had four other three-putts. Take a few of those swings back and you're looking at a stupid low number. What's the takeaway here? Just know that if things were the tiniest bit different you wouldn't be asking me if you can tee-off 15 minutes before twilight starts. Instead, you'd be asking for my autograph.

What to Expect for Your Golfing Dollar

AS A CLUB PRO, I can't remember the last time I pulled out my wallet and paid for golf. It's one of the many benefits that comes with "the life." Most of you aren't that lucky and have to spend your own money to play. Sucks to be you. But as a leading voice in the industry, I think it's important for me to weigh in on what golfers should get for their money.

Public golf courses these days aren't just competing with other golf courses for your dollar, we're also competing against all other leisure activities including, but not limited to, amusement parks, bowling alleys, pickle ball, and Asian massage parlors. I understand that we've got to give consumers something for their dollar. At my course, I preach to the staff, "Give 'em just enough so they come back, not so much that we break our back." That philosophy has always served me well, and my course has a two-star Yelp rating to prove it.

Anyway, the next time you're looking to spend your hard-earned money on a round of golf, here's what you should expect based on the green fee.

Under $25 - You'll see anything on a golf course at this price point (except for a blade of grass): seven-somes, stray dogs, sand greens, missing flagsticks, you name it. It's the trade-off that comes with the freedom to bring coolers on the course, play shirtless, and park the golf carts on the green. At this point you're not really even on a golf course. It's basically an abandoned field where you can hit balls without risking injury to anyone.

$25-$50 - For this price you'd better be getting some basic amenities like a driving range, some type of practice green, gravel cart paths, and a semi-bangable beer-cart girl (excuse me, "beer-cart woman"). You should still expect a couple temp greens, having to race to your ball if you hit it into the wrong fairway before someone else immediately picks it up, and tee boxes that look like they've been carpet bombed, but at least all the golfers on the course will be wearing shoes.

$50-$100 - This is the sweet spot for most of you: cheap enough your wife won't crawl up your ass about the price, well maintained enough so you're not hitting out of divots all day, and expensive enough you can be an absolute prick if anything isn't to your liking. I also want to see working water fountains, not a single temporary green, scorecards that aren't covered in ads like the inside of a Las Vegas taxi cab, and ball washers with water would be nice. You're gonna make some of your money back by filling up your golf bag with free tees, but expect to pay extra for a cart and range balls.

$100 and over - I'm expecting a five-star experience from the minute I hit the parking lot to the moment I leave. They better be "Mr. CPG'ing" me like I just won the goddamned Masters. I don't want to turn my head without seeing some free shit thrown my way: range balls, mouthwash and razors in the locker room, bottles of water in the cart cooler, a moist towel after the round, and all that shit better be included. The range balls should be stacked in a pyramid and the course itself has to be plush. If I see a ball mark on the greens, an unfilled divot in the fairway, or an unraked bunker, you bet your ass they're gonna hear about it when I get in. And I expect luxuries like water features, bridges, an ocean view, an island green, a 700-yard, par-6, or some other high-end design details (what I call "showstoppers.") Last but not least, if it doesn't come with a complimentary bag tag to shove in your buddies' faces when you go home, demand to speak to the GM until they make it right. Trust me, you already paid for it.

Calculating Your True Score

WHEN IT COMES TO scoring, I believe a golfer has three scores on each hole, what you should POST, what you should WRITE DOWN on your card, and what you DESERVED. I call this last one your "True Score®." For an example of True Score®, allow me to refer to this play-by-play from a recent round and you tell me what I shot.

I was playing a 380-yard par-4 and had a $5 Nassau going with one of my junior students. I absolutely smoked my drive down the right side leaving me 160 yards in. I hit a high 7-iron that landed just short of the green and stopped dead without rolling out at all. I then duffed a chip that barely rolled onto the green. Next, I putted it three feet past the hole and then casually one-handed a putt that stopped on the edge. So, what's my score?

I posted a six. I counted my drive, my approach shot, my chip and three putts.

I wrote down a five. I counted my drive, my approach shot, my chip, but only two putts. Before I waved at my last putt, I declared it a gimme assuring me a 5-net-4 and winning the hole.

My True Score® was a four. My drive was perfect, so that's a full stroke. I got pretty screwed on my second shot, which should have taken a big bounce and rolled on the green, leaving me a putt for birdie. I'm pissed about that horrible break and, as a result, I duff my chip so that one doesn't count at all. If I hadn't gotten so screwed on my approach, my first putt would be my birdie putt, so I consider that my third stroke. My three footer is a gimme since an elite player like me is virtually automatic from that distance. So the strokes I count are my drive, my approach shot (which should have ended up on the green), my first putt and a gimme. That's a four in my book.

I preach the three-score system to all my players, and here's a recap of the basics. Always POST the highest POSSIBLE number. Always RECORD the lowest PLAUSIBLE number. Always BRAG to the guys in the grill room about the lowest POSSIBLE number.

Fueling Your Body

EATING RIGHT BEFORE and even during a round of golf is critical for playing your best. As a professional athlete, I learned early on how to make good choices for peak performance, such as: avoiding heavy foods like deep dish pizza for lighter, healthier foods, like thin crust pizza, drinking Zima post-round instead of calorie-heavy beer, and cutting out foods like sushi because raw fish has parasites. All of this should be common knowledge, but sadly, it isn't. If you're on the course without enough calories you can have a lapse in your focus and physical performance. Here's how to eat and drink on the golf course to get the most out of your body.

Scarfing down a huge meal before teeing off is a great way to ensure that your body has enough fuel for the entire round. Back in my mini-tour days, I had a traditional pre-round meal of a Denver omelette, french toast, cookie dough, and a side of bacon. Not only did that give me the energy I needed for five hours of world-class golf, but the bloated feeling that comes with a bulging stomach helped me to feel centered and stable over the ball.

Very few of us have the time or energy to pre-pack an on-course meal, so we eat what's available at the snack bar. Fortunately, golf courses like mine have a bunch of great, healthy options. I recommend eating whole foods with simple ingredients, like a hot dog loaded with veggies like relish and onions. Plain potato chips are good (or another "clean" chip, like Fritos). Pretzels are great. Snickers bars are perfect because they pack a lot of energy that will last you a whole round. Apples are a good choice if you're a real health nut.

Staying hydrated is equally important. Try to stay away from soda (unless it's clear, like Sprite, Mountain Dew, or something juice-based like an orange soda). Drink all the sports drinks you can. They're about the best thing you can put in your body. If you MUST drink alcohol, go with either a light beer or clear liquor and take it easy on the mixers (although a Bloody Mary is good because of the Vitamin C in the tomato juice).

If you race to the course without eating and you're starving, I get it, go ahead and go nuts. Just try to avoid foods that can lead to spills on your clothes. Being hungry on the course sucks, but having a ketchup stain on your Aureus sweater vest is worse!

Avoiding Blow-Up Holes

I'LL ADMIT THAT WHEN I was playing on the Mexican Mini-Tour, no one made more big numbers than me. I chalk it up to my aggressive, "go-for-broke" style of play. No one was less afraid of going low OR going high than me. Because of that, I still hold the all-time tour records for most quads, double-digit scoring holes, and scores that triggered a mandatory post-round verification of my index. As a competitor, I innately understood that the only way to put myself in a position to make a cut late on a Friday afternoon was to take some chances. Blow-up holes are going to happen, but with these tried and true tips, you can keep the damage to a minimum.

1. **Indecision Kills** - When the going gets tough, speed things up. Thinking too much can be a kill-

er on the golf course. If you get into trouble don't think about taking unplayables, picking a safe target, or whether or not you can extract a ball from an impossible lie. Just grab a club, step up, and hit it. Quick decision making prevents you from thinking about all the things that can go wrong and frees you up to let good things happen!

2. **As a General Rule: Go For It -** Every time my trusty caddie Ernesto used to tell me to hit the safe shot I would tell him the same thing, "Players who play it safe, don't get laid and they don't get paid." To play well, you have to throw caution to the wind. Got a tiny opening, tricky lie, or an impossible angle to the hole? Go for it! Think about it. How many times have you had a simple escape shot and still hit it into trouble? My point is, anything can happen on any shot. You're just as likely to pull off an impossible, high-risk shot as you are to botch a simple one. So never, ever take yourself out of a hole with an overly conservative play.

3. **Have a Short Memory -** Making a big number can negatively affect your play for the rest of the round, so it helps to quickly forget and move on. Not only that, it can also be helpful to be forgetful while you're making a big number. Say you're in some knee-deep rough and it takes you three

strokes to get it out. If you zone out while you're chopping away maybe you forget one of those swings and you turn a nine into an eight.

4. **Use the Rule Book -** While I respect the rules of golf "per se," my ignorance of them can be a huge advantage. If you honestly don't know a rule, you can easily break it with a clear conscience. It's like the time I smoked peyote in New Mexico. I honestly had no idea whether it was legal or not, so when I was arrested for public nudity in an Albuquerque Starbucks, I could honestly plead ignorance. The bottom line is you can't call a penalty on yourself if you don't know you did something illegal.

The Most Valuable Chapter in This Book

I'M OFTEN SURPRISED at the number of amateur players I see who stubbornly refuse to carry a ball retriever. I have members here at my club who don't hesitate to buy a demo club or a range pass in order to save a couple bucks, but when it comes to employing a tool that will really save them some money, they act like they're "too cool for school." It's also somewhat ironic that the same guys who are too embarrassed to carry a ball retriever are also the ones who show up to the first tee with a 19 index, outfitted head to toe in bright orange Puma gear.

Honestly, I'm baffled that a golf ball retriever isn't standard issue in EVERY amateur's bag. It's the only club in your arsenal that will literally pay for itself and more. Don't believe me? Check my math.

If you're a 30-year-old player you've got about 50 years of golf ahead of you. If you play twice a month for the rest of your life that's 1,200 rounds. In my experience, a ball retriever is good for finding about a dozen balls per round if, like me, you're willing to completely disregard pace of play and hold up the golfers behind you while fishing for balls. Over the course of your lifetime you'll salvage about 14,400 balls. Considering that an upper tier ball like the Maxfli SoftFli or the Nike Mojo costs about $1.50 per ball, that ball retriever will gross its owner roughly $20,000 over its lifetime. That's enough money to pay the initiation fee at a high-end country club, or get 400 lap dances at Bottoms Up, or three personalized club fittings sessions at Club Champion. Who's laughing now?

Where I Go from Here

As I sit in the kitchen of my condo trying to finish this book, I can't help but notice the Jeff Sluman autographed PAYCHEX hat sitting in a sealed plexiglass case near my refrigerator. I snagged it when Jeff tried to toss it to a little kid in a wheelchair near the rope line at the 1986 Kemper Open. I view it not only as a priceless piece of memorabilia, but also a visible reminder of how blessed I've been throughout my career. Let's face it, there's not very many people out there that can say they've been able to play a "game" for a living and there's not a day that goes by that I don't thank my lucky stars. Now that my glory days as a world-class athlete criss-crossing Mexico are behind me, I look back in awe of all that I accomplished. And while the made cuts, hundreds of dollars won, and a closet full of over 300 free Tobasco/Chiliwear shirts speak volumes, what's really important to me is the legacy I'm leaving behind. So where do I go from here?

On the golf front, I feel like on any given day I'm as dangerous as ever. What can I say, an elite punch out game ages like a fine red wine. I'm consistently shooting 77 to 93 and think a huge breakthrough could be just around the corner. Pending financial backing from a few members here at the club, I'm considering one more run at "the show" on either The Champions Tour or The Señor Tour (the Mexican Champions Tour). If that doesn't work out, I've got my handicap in a place right now where I think I can run off a decade or more of Thursday Night Men's League titles in a row.

As great as my playing career was, I honestly believe my lasting legacy will be Three Jack National (3JN), the championship, semi-private golf course I am building in my hometown of Kansas City, Missouri. It's a labor of love (and a great opportunity to get rich as hell). As I write this I'm collaborating with famed (but troubled) architect Hank Jones on the course design. Despite massive environmental issues and financial mismanagement accusations, I have 100-percent confidence that my baby will be taking the golf world by storm, and I'm not just talking *Golf Digest's* list of America's Best New Courses, I'm talking Top 10 tracks in the world the moment we open the gates.

In addition to 3JN, I also believe this book will be a big part of my legacy. Given my lofty perch in the golf biz, I fully expect it to be an instant classic. Not only will it surely help countless golfers play better and enjoy the game more, but I also believe it will be

THE golf book against which all other golf books are measured. I've read books from Hogan to Penick to Rotella, and I honestly believe this book takes a shit on all of those.

I'm going to get a little sentimental now. The golf course has always been and will always be a sacred place for me. A place to escape. A place where the rules don't apply to me. A place where you can down a 12-pack of Zima and still get behind the wheel of a golf cart. A place where you have the freedom to literally pee anywhere you want. A place where you can push the envelope with married women a little more than you can in a traditional office setting. A place where gambling is not only accepted, but encouraged. In this day and age, places like that are few and far between.

I hope you share the same special feelings about the game that I do. So if you see me on the course, please say, "hello." And if you're lucky enough to play with me, just know I want five a side.

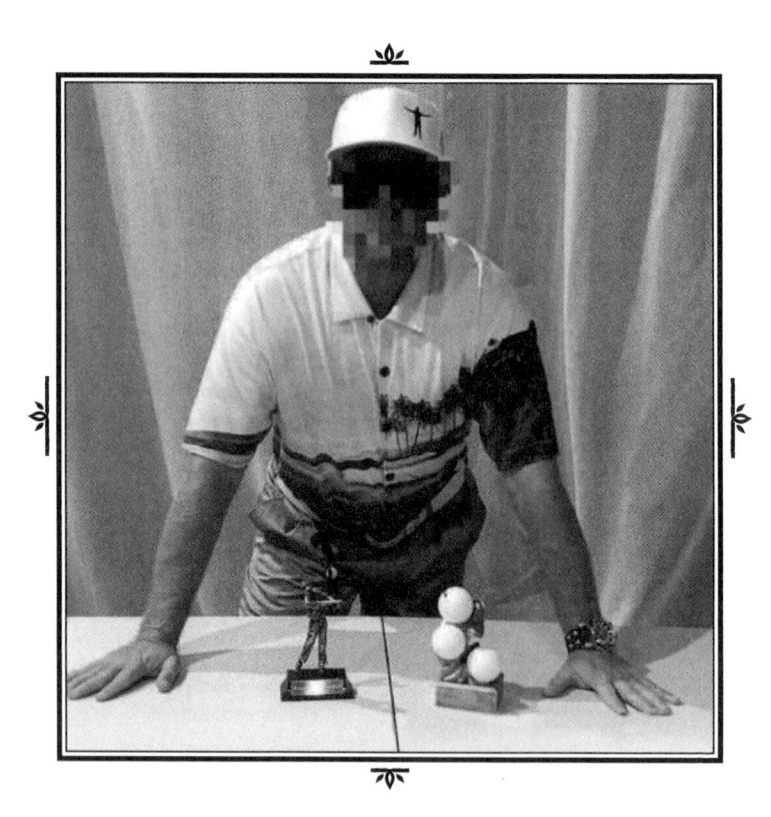

Me, standing with my 1988 Oldsmomobile Scramble Regional Finalist trophy and my 1992 Yucatan Masters "made cut" trophy.

	3/4	FULL	MAX
D		260	
3W	220	190	195
3	208	205	166
4	170	205	200
5	178	170	168
6	167	167	167
7	131	150	136
8	110	150	151
9	129	130	148
9W	118	118	118

	HUNGOVER	FULL	UNDER THE GUN
GW	112	117	131
SW	87	90	126
LW	52	59	112

Oaxaca 3-Tour Challenge
NOTES: 4-11-92

- What's your elbow doing?
- Keep head down until ball lands.
- Don't give a ball to a kid. We only have 4.
- Don't get too high or too low. Stay fairly low at all times.
- Stop noodleing your ball in the fairway. It's a penalty!!
- If you get in contention, hold on tight to the handlebars & steer it home.
- Remind yourself: You probably belong here.
- Both elbows!

1/12 →

*My notations before the 1992 Oaxaca Three-Tour Challenge.
I was always big on preparation.*

Where I'm most at home. Grinding on the range.

My timeshare in Branson. I recharge my batteries here every February 4th and 5th.

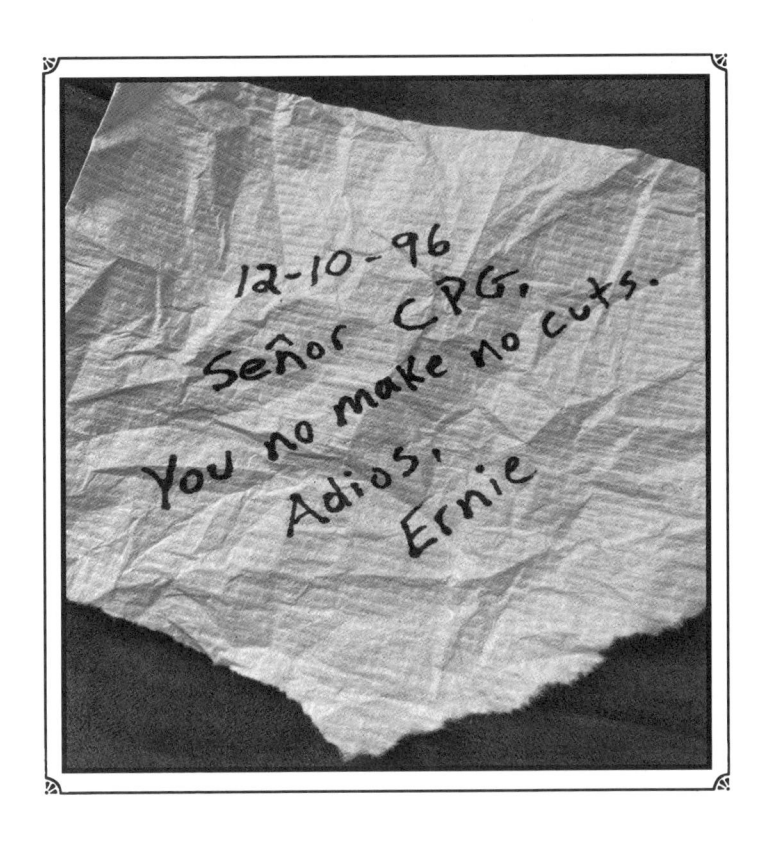

The note my longtime caddie, Ernesto, left me.

Working with PGA Tour player Robert Streb in my Learning Center.

The ball I used when I made the cut on the number at the 1997 Matamoros Four-Ball.

*My home away from home. Bottoms Up.
Love their "Bust a Nut" brunch buffet.*

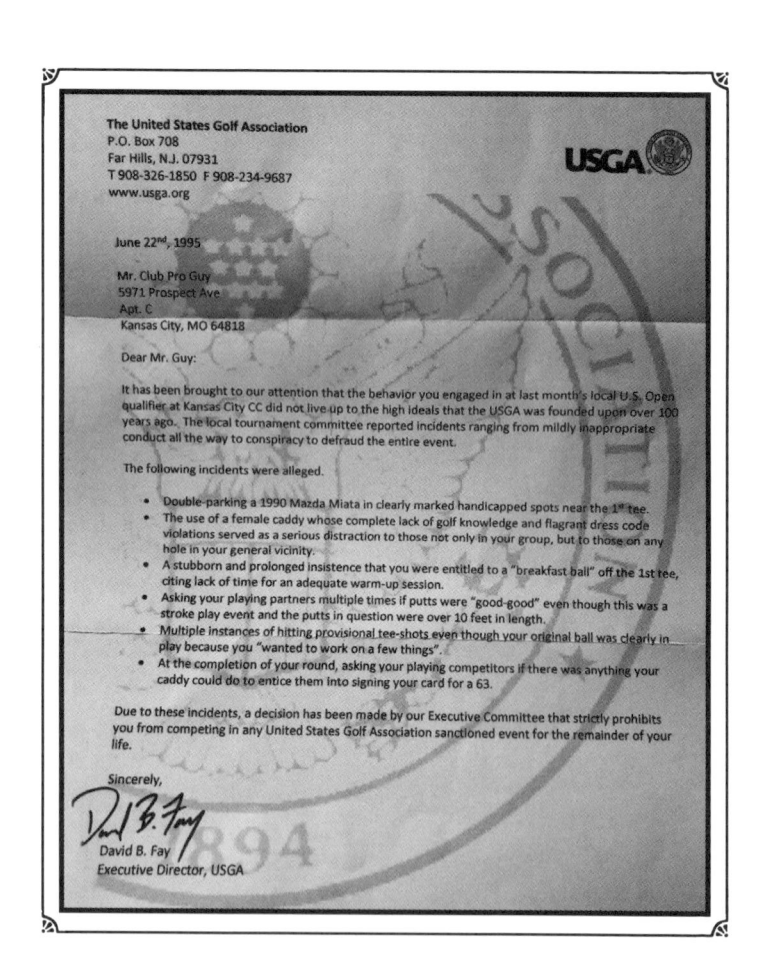

The United States Golf Association
P.O. Box 708
Far Hills, N.J. 07931
T 908-326-1850 F 908-234-9687
www.usga.org

June 22nd, 1995

Mr. Club Pro Guy
5971 Prospect Ave
Apt. C
Kansas City, MO 64818

Dear Mr. Guy:

It has been brought to our attention that the behavior you engaged in at last month's local U.S. Open qualifier at Kansas City CC did not live up to the high ideals that the USGA was founded upon over 100 years ago. The local tournament committee reported incidents ranging from mildly inappropriate conduct all the way to conspiracy to defraud the entire event.

The following incidents were alleged.

- Double-parking a 1990 Mazda Miata in clearly marked handicapped spots near the 1st tee.
- The use of a female caddy whose complete lack of golf knowledge and flagrant dress code violations served as a serious distraction to those not only in your group, but to those on any hole in your general vicinity.
- A stubborn and prolonged insistence that you were entitled to a "breakfast ball" off the 1st tee, citing lack of time for an adequate warm-up session.
- Asking your playing partners multiple times if putts were "good-good" even though this was a stroke play event and the putts in question were over 10 feet in length.
- Multiple instances of hitting provisional tee-shots even though your original ball was clearly in play because you "wanted to work on a few things".
- At the completion of your round, asking your playing competitors if there was anything your caddy could do to entice them into signing your card for a 63.

Due to these incidents, a decision has been made by our Executive Committee that strictly prohibits you from competing in any United States Golf Association sanctioned event for the remainder of your life.

Sincerely,

David B. Fay
Executive Director, USGA

The infamous 1995 letter I received from the USGA.

Me, standing on the site of what will be Three Jack National, a championship, semi-private golf course, and most likely... my lasting legacy.